RAGE

Sarah M[illegible] & Co.

COURAGE

Coaches & Entrepreneurs Share Their Stories of Struggle and Their Strategies For *Success*

ISBN: 9798340915474

Legal Notice:

This book is for personal use only. You cannot amend, distribute, sell, use, quote or paraphrase any part of this book's content without the author's or copyright owner's consent. Legal action will be pursued if this is breached. The information provided herein is stated to be truthful and consistent in that any liability, in terms of inattention or otherwise, by any usage or abuse of any policies, processes, or directions contained within is the solitary and utter responsibility of the recipient reader. Under no circumstances will any legal responsibility or blame be held against the publisher for any reparation, damages, or monetary loss due to the information herein, either directly or indirectly.

Disclaimer Notice:

The views, opinions, and advice expressed by other authors in this book are solely their own.

This book is not providing medical advice; it is intended for informational purposes only. It is not a substitute for professional medical advice, diagnosis or treatment. Never ignore professional medical advice in seeking treatment. Every attempt has been made to provide accurate, up-to-date, reliable, and complete information. No warranties of any kind are expressed or implied. Readers acknowledge that the author is not engaging in the rendering of legal, financial, medical or professional advice. By reading this document, the reader agrees that under no circumstances are we responsible for any losses, direct or indirect, which are incurred as a result of the use of the information contained within this document, including, but not limited to, errors, omissions, or inaccuracies.

These stories are written by real people in their own words.

DEDICATION

Quite simply, this book is dedicated to anyone who ***has, is,***

and ***will*** *experience mental health challenges.*

My hope is that in this book you will…

Find the strength and encouragement you might be looking for.

Find the light that you need in a time that might be feeling so dark.

Find the connections at a point in your life that might be feeling lonely.

You are in my thoughts, always and forever.

Sarah x

"Don't ever lose hope because better days will come." Ana Monnar

Important: This book might be triggering as it contains stories about self harm, abuse and traumatic experiences. I urge you to use your discretion when reading. If you feel triggered, or your circumstances are so desperate that you require additional support. Please do reach out to someone in your network, or other professional services that can support you. Some of these services include but are not limited to:

Mind: www.mind.org.uk/need-urgent-help/using-this-tool/

Samaritans: www.samaritans.org/how-we-can-help/if-youre-having-difficult-time/

Mental Health America: www.mhanational.org/

CONTENTS

FOREWORD

By Sarah Makinde

After experiencing the huge shock and upset of two people in my wider community and friendship group taking their own lives, the sadness was overwhelming. The circumstances that led to their death, and the images of when I last saw them seemingly enjoying life, consumed my thoughts. I just couldn't imagine what it must feel like to be hiding that pain behind a smile, and yet behind it all, thinking that there was no other way out. It was devastating - so many unanswered questions and 'what ifs.'

This experience and my own battles with mental health, where I felt so desperate, so alone and so overwhelmed led me to a lifelong search to develop more knowledge in the area of mental wellbeing. I knew that if

I was better able to understand other people's and my own mental health, this would help me to know how to make a bigger difference.

Not long into my quest for more information, I found compelling research on the importance of connections with others, and the role that strong relationships have on our mental wellbeing. I have always enjoyed connecting with others, but this research gave me a new meaning to connection, not just for business, or for enjoyment, but to literally save lives.

Last year I decided to not just look for information, but to start connecting with others to talk about my own mental health journey. As part of this desire to connect, I had the opportunity to be part of a wonderful book collaboration project, which soon became my outlet for one particular mental health challenge that I thought I had let go of, but soon found out I hadn't.

What I discovered as part of this journey, is that when I started to connect and share my own journey with my mental health struggles, it created a ripple effect. When people read my story, they would contact me directly to open up and share their own. It was so powerful.

Writing the chapter in the book allowed me to revisit those moments in my life that were really dark. I realised during the writing process that mental health challenges and things I thought I had long forgotten, and that I felt were no longer impacting me or part of my life, were just merely hiding in the dark corner of a room in my mind, ready to come out again! This can happen to keep us safe and to enable us to keep functioning, but at the end of the day, these thoughts, feelings and emotions can still be there, just waiting to come up again.

When I shared my story in the book, not only did it help others to share theirs, but it became cathartic. It was an opportunity to not just take me back to that moment to release the traumatic thoughts, feelings and emotion, but at the same time it helped me realise just how far I had come. It enabled me to let go of the energy that had been unknowingly trapped at that time.

The feeling I experienced when I let go sparked a strong desire to help others experience a similar feeling of freedom. To give people an opportunity to share their own stories that impacted their mental health. This was all with the hope that they would rediscover the strength and courage they might not have even realised they had at that time to get through it, and at the same time also realise how far they had come. My dream was that their stories would then inspire and encourage others who might be experiencing something similar with no way of yet knowing that things can get better.

Courage is an eclectic mix of real life stories about mental health from a variety of authors with very diverse backgrounds. These stories are woven together to create a wonderful tapestry of experiences. The stories are so unique across every chapter - this supports the fact that mental health does not discriminate. It touches everyone, whether this is directly or indirectly regardless of gender, age, cultural background, economic situations, status…the list goes on!

COURAGE

There are many books with many stories about mental health. I wanted our book to not just be about sharing information, but about real life stories that give hope and offer support when you might need it most. Like in those moments where you might be feeling like shutting yourself away from the world, or not feeling like you can reach out to anyone - ***Courage*** and we are here for you.

"Courage doesn't always roar. Sometimes courage is the little voice at the end of the day that says I'll try again tomorrow." — Mary Anne Radmacher

COURAGE

"MENTAL HEALTH DOES NOT DISCRIMINATE—IT TOUCHES EVERY LIFE, REVEALING BOTH THE FRAGILITY AND STRENGTH WITHIN US ALL. IN THE KALEIDOSCOPE OF OUR EXPERIENCES, IT'S NOT THE CHALLENGES THAT DEFINE US, BUT THE COURAGE WE FIND TO RISE ABOVE THEM."

– SARAH MAKINDE

CHAPTER 1

Finding Me Again

By Sarah Makinde

Putting Out Fires

During the early stages of reaching out to people to collaborate on this book, I had an epiphany. I was stuck in traffic when I saw a fire engine go past. Emblazoned on the side was the message "fire does not discriminate." It struck me that mental health is the same—mental health challenges do not discriminate in any kind of way. Males aged 45 to 49 have the highest age-specific suicide rate (ONS). Rates among under 25s have generally increased in recent years. Mental health touches everyone, whether directly or indirectly. Society has become more open to talking about it, but it always feels like more needs to be done to help people recognize the signs, support them in crises, and prevent lives from being lost.

We see it all the time—people who on the surface appear to have everything, yet in the next breath, we hear of their crises, anguish, and sometimes loss of life. As a self-confessed empath, it literally breaks my heart to know that someone is going through this and unable to speak out. I believe that we can never truly understand what another person is going through. While we can try to empathise, we don't share the same values, beliefs, upbringing, or thought patterns, and thus cannot feel exactly what someone else is feeling. All I know is that I've been there with mental health struggles, including anxiety, overwhelm, and periods of deep depression. For me, it felt like trying—very unsuccessfully—to put out the fires. When I managed to pour water on one, another would ignite somewhere else in my life. At times, it felt never-ending.

There were many occasions when I wore a 'brave' face and just kept my head down, getting on with things while feeling like I was literally dying inside. Times when I struggled massively, yet to the world, I appeared fine.

As a parent, coach, and someone responsible for many people and teams for over 20 years, my life often revolved around looking after others at the expense of myself. It somehow felt wrong to put myself first, so I ended up putting myself last, perhaps even losing myself in the process.

My story is about how I lost who I was in these moments of crisis, upset, and people-pleasing. Yet, in these same moments, it is also about how I found the courage to be brave, to fight through, and to become me—the version of me I truly wanted to be, not who the world told me to be.

The Kaleidoscope Effect

As I sit here and begin to write this chapter, I realise that mental health struggles have infiltrated every part of my life and continue to do so. To tell you just one part of my story would not do my mental health journey justice. It would only scratch the surface of sharing tools and tips that could help others in similar situations.

My mental health journey—and my life—can only be described as a kaleidoscope. Rich in colour, full of twists and turns, and with every shift, a new picture is created. I have countless stories of desperation, despair, courage, and what I can only describe as miracles. There are so many that I could write a whole book on them, but we'll save that for another time.

This chapter is a glimpse into these stories, shortened to extract the key learnings from my experiences. I also share the tools that have helped me through each mental health challenge. Mental health challenges can sometimes feel like being a helpless ship tossed about by a rough sea, battling the elements with everything feeling out of control. In times like this, the phrases, affirmations, or quotes I will share have acted as my anchor—a consistent reminder that we are stronger than we think, and that these hard times and rough seas will not last forever—it too shall pass.

This is where my story begins…

It All Started With The Labels

Someone once said to me, "What other people think of us is none of our business." But I had made it my business for so many years. I let what other people thought of me dictate everything—my thoughts, feelings, and emotions. It wasn't until I stopped doing this that what people thought of me mattered less, and what I thought of myself became the priority. To get to this point, I need to take you back to some key moments in my life.

I am of mixed heritage, I was born in Nigeria and then moved to the UK. For most of my life, I felt like I never really fit in anywhere. I got pregnant at a young age and was labelled by society as a teenage mum who would never amount to much. I left home at 15 years old and was labelled 'average' at every parent's evening I can remember. My mixed heritage even meant that some people struggled to label me, and I didn't fit into any box created.

Revisiting my past, it's no wonder I spent years feeling exhausted, depressed, and lonely. I spent half my life feeling confused, lost, and battling against labels that either others gave me or I imposed on myself. Labels like "I am not good enough," "I will never be enough," or "There is something wrong with me." These labels influenced every area of my life—my ability to feel happy, loved, and wanted. It's no surprise that these labels became part of my ongoing battle with mental health.

The Uphill Struggle

My whole life from around the age of 6 years old felt like an uphill struggle. Growing up in a place where everyone seemed so different to me, going through my teenage pregnancy, leaving home, and almost failing school created an obsession to prove people wrong about the labels associated with these events. Society told me daily, through comments, looks, and reactions, that I wasn't going to be successful. But I was determined to succeed, regardless of the cost. What it took was being sick and running to the toilet while pregnant and studying for my A-levels, staying up all night with Red Bull while caring for my young child and attending university, taking on five cleaning jobs while trying to buy a house and doing my master's, doing free consulting while starting my business and studying for a doctorate in psychology and so many sacrifices. Lost time with my son and family, working late and having no life what-so-ever, and sacrificing who I wanted to be for who I thought I should be.

Everyone I tell this story to always says I must feel proud of my achievements and they admire the sacrifices, hard work and effort. I always felt confused by this 'proud' comment. A sense of pride, to me, meant accomplishment. I didn't feel proud because I always felt like I hadn't accomplished anything. This was because I did it all to prove to others that I was enough and to challenge the label. I never did it for myself—I didn't feel happy, satisfied, or loved doing it. By striving harder, I just ended up losing myself, feeling miserable, and feeling even less than enough.

Comparisonitis Creates Dis-ease

"Comparison is the thief of joy." (Theodore Roosevelt)

From all this, you might guess that I know what it's like to feel different—to be a minority in a place full of the majority. Walking into an office or a room and looking different from everyone else, or being the only teenage mum, or immigrant, or female in a male dominated room. I remember once in the work canteen, a lady said she loved my tan. I was so embarrassed as it was in front of my colleagues. At the time, I laughed it off, knowing it was an innocent comment, but it deepened my awareness of my differences and inability to fit in. I've even been asked if I have Botox in my lips, told my hair looks more professional when straightened rather than in its natural state, and heard derogatory comments from my friends about immigration. All of this affected my mental health, self-esteem, and my obsession with comparing myself to those who looked and sounded very different from me. I wanted to be more like them.

I grew up and spent much of my early adult years telling myself I would never be as pretty, popular, or brave as others. Whatever word you use to fill in the following sentence "I will never be as [................] as them", it all stems from the same disease—comparisonitis! I couldn't see the value I added by simply being me. The truth is, I didn't actually know who ME was! I straightened my hair, not because I wanted to, but because others said it looked more 'professional.' I spoke in a certain way so people would think I was capable of doing a certain job. I completely lost who I was.

What I didn't realise was that by trying to please everyone, I wasn't pleasing anyone—least of all myself. I was absolutely miserable. I was like an actor in my own life—smiling to play a character but not knowing who I really was.

Mindfulness Was the Difference That Made the Difference

I thought mindfulness would help me get rid of those negative automatic thoughts (NATS)—to escape from them. What I learned instead was how to allow those thoughts to be there, to bring awareness to them, and notice without judgement. When I started to notice my thoughts and emotions, rather than escaping from them, I welcomed them. I realised that my emotions and thoughts are not me. By noticing them, I was able to let them pass. Thoughts of not being enough, of being a failure, of being different.

It took me a long time to understand that I am not my emotions, and my emotions are not me. It might feel like it during challenging times. It is an experience and a sensation. Experience it and let it pass. When I learned cognitive behavioural hypnotherapy, the trainer said something that stuck with me: "We hypnotise ourselves every day. We give ourselves suggestions that we can't do something or that we are not good enough. Why not hypnotise ourselves for good—telling ourselves that we can do something and that we are good enough?" These tools have saved me so many times from my mind.

I don't know about you, but I am definitely an overthinker. Within minutes, my mind can create a multitude of stories, solutions, alternatives, and possibilities. Even knowing about unhelpful thinking styles doesn't stop the 'mindreading,' 'black and white thinking,' or 'catastrophizing.' It just helps me create awareness and take action, such as taking a pause and going back to mindful breathing.

Mental Health Doesn't Discriminate

Finally, I'm still surprised when I see someone who seems to have it all—wealth, status, success, relationships—yet still battles with mental health. I used to think I'd be happy and free from mental health challenges if I achieved certain things or had a certain status. What I now realise is that everyone has their battles, and mental health doesn't discriminate. Whether you're famous, a single parent, a CEO, or just a regular person, everyone can experience mental health issues.

This realisation has changed how I approach my mental health. It has given me a sense of solidarity and understanding that we all have our struggles and that there's no shame in reaching out for support. As they say, it's okay to not be okay, and it's okay to ask for help.

The Moment The Dots Connected

***"What is to give light must endure burning."* Viktor Frankl.**

It is through this journey that my business was born - like the phoenix rising from the ashes. When I look back, I now realise that every trial, tribulation and path I have travelled down, has contributed towards the passion I now have to help people who have either been in similar situations, or who just don't believe they are enough and struggle with their mental health because of this.

In the last 12 months I have grown my business to 6 figures, created a Facebook community of over 16,000 people, started a joint venture business, and purchased another property that I am currently renovating. It still amazes me how by not accepting the labels that I mentioned at the beginning of this chapter, meant that things turned out very different to the statistics that could have dictated my destiny.

Whilst I am now able to feel that sense of achievement. More than this, I am clear on who I am - I have a voice, I value and appreciate myself and my journey and I trust, whilst it can be difficult to see it at the time, that all things work together for good. Even the times that push me to my limits and seem like a never-ending battle. The next day can feel very different.

My biggest learning from my journey so far, is that self-acceptance is everything. Yes, I am a teenage mum, and by growing through this experience it has taught me resilience, tenacity and the ability to be flexible.

This is not my name, this is part of my history and what makes me able to relate to people who have gone through struggles, who are balancing so much, who are experiencing judgement by others for whatever reasons.

All these moments in my life have without a shadow of a doubt brought me to the place I am in today, and have contributed to the person I am today. I am so grateful for them.

The 'One Wish' Question

So, if you're feeling overwhelmed or struggling, know that you are not alone. I hope that by sharing my journey and the tools that have helped me, you might find some comfort and guidance. Mental health is a lifelong journey, and while we may not always have all the answers, we can always keep moving forward. Remember, you are stronger than you think, and there is always hope, even in the darkest of times.

In coaching, we often ask our clients - "if you had one wish, what would that be?" My wish for everyone is that they see their struggle as their strength. That they know that they are enough. That they feel loved, wanted and appreciated. This is my wish for you.

Connect with me…

I am a Chartered Psychologist, Master Strengths Coach & NLP Trainer. I'm passionate about using evidence based psychological tools and techniques to provide ethical coaching, consulting, learning and development services to individuals and to corporate businesses.

If you are a coach, trainer, or consultant and would like to access coaching, or further support and free workshops I would love you to join my community of over 16,000 people in **The Coaching Corner: www.facebook.com/groups/thecoachingcorner**

CHAPTER 2

By Lucie Reveco

NLP Trainer, Therapist and Professional Coach

to brave women who want to find home within

Finding Home Within

As Dr. Gabor Maté says "Trauma is not what happens to us, it's what happens inside us as a result of what happened to us." After overcoming childhood physical abuse trauma that caused me bulimia and unhealthy anger issues I realised that what happened to me was not my fault, but it was my fault that I ran away from it, hid it and refused to deal with it for so many years. Until I was thirty-three, I thought I was broken. I then came to realise that there was nothing wrong with me at all; the trauma disconnected me from my body, and I could not hear my inner wisdom. The hardest thing I needed to do was to overcome my fear of not knowing and replace it with courage to walk the healing path to my wholeness, to reconnect my head with my heart and inner wisdom. I had to stop fighting, punishing myself and controlling everything and everyone. Now at the age of thirty-nine, I know that I needed to surrender and accept my deep inner wounds to be able to hear my inner wisdom again. I learned from Dr. Maté that trauma is the invisible force that shaped my life. It shaped the way I live, the way I love and the way I make sense of the world…and I decided to change it…

The Shadows of Childhood

The first rays of dawn pierced through the windows of the big and cold house, revealing the scars of the past etched into the walls and floorboards. It was in this house that I had spent the first twelve years of my life, a life that, from an outside perspective, might have seemed extraordinary. But beneath the surface, hidden behind closed doors and forced smiles, lay a world of pain and suffering. I was a bright and very gentle spirited child, my laughter ringing out like the clear chime of a bell. I had a wild imagination, always dreaming up fantastical worlds where I could escape the harsh realities of my existence. For me, the days were a blur of fear and uncertainty, punctuated by moments of violence that left me trembling in the darkness of my room that I shared with my younger sister.

My father, a man of imposing stature and a volatile temper, had turned our home into a hellish prison. The reasons for his anger were as unpredictable as they were numerous: a dish left unwashed, a toy misplaced, a wrong answer to an innocent question. A man who loved alcohol and pubs more than his own family. I learned quickly to tiptoe around him, to become as invisible as possible, hoping to avoid the next outburst. But no amount of caution could completely shield me from his wrath. My mother, a kind, caring but very weak woman, seemed to retreat further into herself with each passing day. She bore her own scars, both physical and emotional, and her shouting became a cocoon in which she hid her pain. I yearned for my mother's embrace, for words of comfort and reassurance, but they were rarely given. Instead, she found her own release at punishing me and my sister. My sister and I became their servants who had to be "good girls", be quiet, listen to all orders like to go to sleep at 6pm, or wake up and eat at 2am, clean and scrub the mess that the drunk father created at 3am. I witnessed all of the terrifying things that my father did to my mother, from locking her outside in the cold just in her pyjamas, barefoot, drowning her in the toilet or cracking eggs or ceramic dishes on her head. I was so scared, and I thought he would kill us one day. I still remember the fear and anger that was building inside me for twelve years until I found the inner strength to speak up and face him. So I did. I got us out of the prison to start again…

Battling the Demons Within Abroad

Desperation led me to a decision that would change the course of my life. At the age of nineteen, with nothing but a small suitcase and a heart full of unresolved pain, I decided to leave. I had heard stories of people finding themselves in far-off lands, of discovering new versions of themselves amidst unfamiliar cultures and landscapes. And so, with a mix of fear and determination, I sat on the bus to the United Kingdom. The journey abroad was both exhilarating and terrifying. I found myself in a bustling city, its streets alive with the sounds of a language I didn't understand. I took on odd jobs and the role of an au-pair to support myself, each day a new challenge that pushed me out of my comfort zone. The anonymity of being in a foreign place provided a strange comfort; I could reinvent myself, free from the shadows of my past. In this new land, I began to explore the depths of my soul, but the weight of my trauma became a heavy burden. My once joyful spirit was slowly eroded by self-doubt and self-loathing. I became a shadow of the girl I once was, my days marked by a growing sense of worthlessness. In my twenties, this internal struggle manifested in the form of bulimia. I sought control in the only way I knew how: through the meticulous and destructive cycle of bingeing and purging. The bulimia was a dark secret, hidden behind closed bathroom doors and carefully timed meals. It provided a perverse sense of control, a way to numb the pain and quiet the voices in my head that told me I wasn't good enough. But with each passing day, the cycle became harder to break, and the toll it took on my body and mind was devastating.

For five long years, I battled with my eating disorder. My reflection in the mirror became an enemy, a constant reminder of my perceived failures. I hated myself. I felt trapped in a vicious cycle, unable to see a way out. The walls of my childhood home, once a place of fear, now seemed to close in on me, suffocating my soul.

Embracing Strength Through Adversity

As I immersed myself in my university studies and embarked on my career path, I found solace in academic pursuits and professional achievements. The demanding nature of my studies and the challenges of my chosen field provided a welcome distraction from the tumultuous emotions that had long plagued me. I threw myself into my work with a relentless determination, channelling my energy into achieving excellence and carving out a niche for myself in my chosen field. My journey through university was not just an academic pursuit but a personal odyssey of reclaiming my sense of self-worth and identity. The structured environment of lectures and deadlines offered a sense of stability and purpose, helping to anchor me in moments of uncertainty. Dedication and hard work were met with recognition and success, fuelling my ambition to excel even further.

In my pursuit of professional success, I found myself adopting what I described as an "ice queen" persona—a shield of self-preservation forged from masculine energy. This persona, characterised by a cool demeanour and a focus on efficiency, became my armour against the vulnerabilities that lingered beneath the surface. It allowed me to navigate the competitive world of a corporate company and later, the professional realm, with a sense of detachment that shielded me from emotional entanglements.

However, amidst my academic and professional achievements, I found myself ensnared in toxic relationships that tested my newfound strength. I became entangled with men who sought to possess me without offering commitment or respect. The scars of my past made me vulnerable to manipulation, and I found myself drawn into a tumultuous affair with a married man—a decision that left me grappling with guilt and self-doubt.

It was in the midst of this turmoil that I made the bold decision to leave England and return to my native Czech Republic. The move was a pivotal moment of self-realisation and empowerment. It represented a reclaiming of my autonomy and a refusal to be defined by destructive patterns of behaviour. I knew that true healing required a physical and emotional distance from the toxic environments and relationships that had held me captive.

Returning to the Czech Republic was not just a geographical relocation but a symbolic homecoming—a return to my roots and a reconnection with my inner strength. It was a decision fuelled by a deep-seated desire to break free from the chains of my past and to forge a new path towards healing and self-discovery.

As I settled back into familiar surroundings, I began the process of unravelling the layers of pain and self-doubt that had accumulated over the years. I sought therapy and surrounded myself with supportive friends and family who encouraged me on my journey of healing. Gradually, I learned to soften the edges of my "ice queen" persona, embracing vulnerability as a source of strength rather than weakness. Through introspection and self-reflection, I emerged stronger and more resilient than ever before. I recognised the importance of setting boundaries and prioritising my own well-being, refusing to settle for relationships or situations that compromised my values and self-respect. My journey towards healing and self-empowerment was far from linear, but it was marked by courage, resilience, and an unwavering determination to reclaim my sense of worth and identity.

The Healing Path to Wholeness

As I delved deeper into yoga and meditation, I discovered a newfound strength within myself. The poses that had once seemed impossible became attainable with time and patience. I learned to appreciate my body for what it could do, rather than criticise it for perceived imperfections. The practice became a form of meditation, a way to quiet the noise in my mind and focus on the present moment. Through yoga and self-journaling I also found a deeper connection to the concept of self-love. I began to understand that healing was not about erasing the past, but about accepting it and finding ways to move forward. I learned to forgive myself for the years of self-hate and destructive behaviour, recognising that they were coping mechanisms born from immense pain. This journey of self-acceptance was neither quick nor easy, but it was profoundly transformative.

As the months turned into years, I continued to grow and heal. I thought I'd healed, and I was so happy. I fell in love, married and gave life to two beautiful children. But the moment that I became a mother my unhealthy anger started to bubble up again.. I was angry all the time, I could not stop the aggression and I started to fear myself and my actions. I was worried about my little boy. I was worried that I would hurt him, which I did several times. I felt like a monster who was yelling and hurting my innocent and loving son, and I knew I was causing him trauma. My marriage was in danger and my husband was powerless to help. I sought help but the psychologist's interventions were not the right tools for me. I did not want to repeat and relive my childhood trauma again and again. I did not want to destroy myself from the pain, and I needed to function as a mother of a baby boy. I enrolled in NLP and coaching training to help myself, wanting to know the answers to my questions. Neuro Linguistic programming had tools to reframe my pain and replace my unwanted toxic behaviour with supportive ones. I vividly recall my first conversation with my coach and close friend, Steve, who said to me: "Stop being so harsh on yourself, switch your head off and connect to your body…you will be fine." This sentence changed my life. I knew that acceptance of my situation and healing was a journey, and I was on the right track. I exchanged fear for love, fighting for surrender, and anger for humour. Here I am now, a professional coach and an international certified NLP trainer who is helping you to reconnect within. Influenced by Dr. Gabor Maté and Dr. Milton Erickson, who helped me to understand my pain, I am in turn helping my clients to understand theirs.

Throughout my journey, I never forgot the family I had left behind. I stayed in touch with my mother and sister through sporadic visits and phone calls, slowly rebuilding the fragile bridge of our relationship. My biological father remained a distant figure, his presence a ghostly reminder of the pain I had endured. But I knew that true healing required facing the past head-on, and so I made the difficult decision to heal and return home through hypnotherapy to forgive my father.

Coming Full Circle

I had built a new life for myself, one filled with love, growth, and a sense of purpose. But I also knew that part of my healing journey involved confronting my past, not running from it. The old house stood as a testament to the passage of time, its walls bearing witness to both the horrors of the past and the potential for new beginnings. My heart pounded in my chest as I approached the front door, memories flooding back with each step. I stepped inside, enveloped in a hesitant embrace that spoke volumes. The house felt different, both familiar and foreign, a place where old wounds could be acknowledged, and new memories could be created. The house was owned by someone else. I was relieved that the suffering was over. My mother with her new husband, and my little stepbrother had built a new home.

The reunion with my mother was a mix of tears and laughter, of shared stories and unspoken apologies. We talked late into the night, our conversation a tapestry of pain and healing. I learned more about my mother's own struggles, about the cycle of abuse that had shaped our lives. There were no easy answers or quick fixes, but there was a sense of mutual understanding and a desire to move forward together. I decided not to confront my father. I decided not to see him ever again. I approached my trauma with a mix of fear and determination, and I am still not ready to face the man who had caused me so much pain. I realised that true closure did not depend on his words, but on my own ability to let go of the anger and resentment that had bound me for so long.

I dedicated myself to raising awareness about childhood abuse trauma and eating disorders, helping people to overcome their pain as a therapist, coach and NLP trainer. I founded **www.reveco.me** to empower and support women on their own healing journeys. My story, once a source of shame, became a beacon of hope for others who had faced similar struggles. My voice, once silenced by fear, now resonated with compassion and resilience.

Through my work, I found a renewed sense of purpose. I saw the ripple effect of my healing, how my journey had the power to touch and transform the lives of others. The pain of my past was not forgotten, but it no longer defined me. Instead, it became a source of strength, a reminder of the incredible resilience of the human spirit.

As the years went by, my life blossomed in ways I had never imagined. I found love with a partner who cherished and respected me, who supported me in my mission to help others. Together, we built a life filled with laughter, adventure, and a deep sense of connection. My heart, once heavy with the weight of my past, now overflowed with gratitude and joy. My relationship with my mother continued to heal, our bond growing stronger with each passing day. We supported each other through the ups and downs of life, our shared experiences creating a foundation of understanding and empathy. My biological father remained a distant figure, but there was a sense of peace in knowing that I had faced my past and emerged stronger.

In quiet moments of reflection, I often think back to the girl I once was. I remember the fear and pain, the years of self-hate and struggle. But I also see the incredible journey I have undertaken, and the transformation that has occurred within me. I have found my way back to myself, to a place of love and acceptance.

My story is one of resilience and redemption, a testament to the power of the human spirit to overcome even the darkest of circumstances. I have faced my past with courage, embraced my present with compassion, and look towards the future with hope. In finding myself, I have also found a way to help others, to be a beacon of light in a world that often feels overshadowed by darkness.

And so, my journey continues, a never-ending path of growth and self-discovery. I know that life will always present challenges, but I also know that I possess the strength to face them. With each step, I move forward with a heart full of love and a spirit unbroken, ready to embrace whatever the future holds.

Let my story be the catalyst for your own transformation, guiding you towards a life filled with self-love, strength, and the unwavering belief that you deserve happiness and peace. "Finding Home Within" is more than a story; it is a movement towards healing and empowerment for women everywhere. Embrace your journey and find your home within. If you enjoyed my story, let's get connected:

Website: www.reveco.me

Facebook / Instagram / LinkedIn:

www.linktr.ee/luciereveco

CHAPTER 3

Rising Above the Ashes: my Phoenix Journey

By Dr Suzanne Henwood

Everything changes in a flash

I was on a real high as I flew home from a health conference after an exhilarating weekend. Life couldn't have been better—I had recently settled into living amongst the stunning landscape of New Zealand, secured an enviable position as an Associate Professor, and was surrounded by a close-knit family. We were all healthy, thriving, and basking in the glow of our new adventure.

And then, in an instant, everything changed.

I lost everything.

As I was about to drive home from the airport, my phone rang. It was my neighbour. *"Where are you?"* he asked. I thought, *"How odd, he's never called before. Who gave him my number?"*

His next words shattered my world: *"Flames are coming out of your house, and I don't know where your family is."*

Time froze. The next few minutes were a blur. An adrenaline surge coursed through my veins. My mind went blank, my heart pounded in my throat, and nausea twisted my stomach. Fear, anxiety, and panic washed over me, leaving my body tingling all over. I was feeling, rather than hearing, the message. I put the phone down, and all I could think was, *"Is this really happening?"*

I took a deep breath—one of those long, slow exhales I often teach my clients—and sighed. I knew I had to get home, but I had to get there safely. I called my husband, but there was no answer. I called my daughter who told me she was at a youth club—Phew! I called my son, and again, no answer. Out of options, I took another long, slow breath to steady myself. I had to focus. Random thoughts raced through my mind: *"What would I find? Was my family safe? Why hadn't I asked my neighbour if he'd called the fire service?"*

I imagined my house engulfed in flames or burned to the ground, my family trapped inside, my poor cats trapped, helpless…

It's remarkable what you focus on in a crisis. It wasn't images of my work, valuables, favourite shoes or family heirlooms that flashed through my mind, but those things linked to my values—what was truly important to me- that flashed through my mind. In that moment, all that mattered was getting home and finding out if my family was okay.

As realization set in

As I drove up the road towards home, the darkness enveloping me, flashing lights blocked the path ahead. Panic surged within me. I rushed to the fire crew, desperate to get through, telling them *"It's my house that's on fire!"* The crew calmly instructed me to park and walk from here.

What on earth was I about to find? My heart pounded wildly, my stomach churned with nausea, and my body felt as though it were ablaze, tingling uncontrollably. I locked the car, my mind racing irrationally with thoughts about whether my luggage and laptop would be safe in the car. The adrenaline scattered my thoughts, a chaotic whirlwind of fear and confusion.

As I began to walk towards the inferno my teenage son ran towards me and barrelled into my arms. Barefoot and clad in a onesie, he looked like a Big Bear hurtling towards me. In that moment, my focus shifted entirely. This was about showing up, calm, collected and regulated for my kids. I held him tightly, offering reassurance through touch. There were no words, I simply held him. I didn't know yet that he had discovered the fire.

Together, arm in arm, we walked towards the house.

The scene was overwhelming. The noise deafening—people shouting, wood popping and cracking, and then, a window blew out with a thunderous explosion. I struggled to process the chaos as another window shattered in a fiery burst.

I spotted my husband in the chaos. There were no words—just a profound, wordless connection, soul to soul. He wrapped his arms around me, and in that embrace, I felt a flicker of reassurance. We were safe. We would face this together, finding our way through the unknown. We were on an unexpected path, and though we had no idea what lay ahead, I knew we would navigate it side by side.

My neighbour arrived with coats, his familiar presence a small comfort in the storm of uncertainty. He reassured us of his support as we stood, lost and waiting for direction. Helpless, with no idea of what to do next, we realized we were no longer in control. Our home—our sanctuary, our family fortress—was gone. Everything had shifted in that one devastating evening. All we could do was wait, and the waiting was agonizing.

Time slowed to a crawl, stretching each moment into an eternity.

Hours later, the flames had been extinguished, but the smoke still lingered, wrapping around us like a shroud. It burned at the back of my throat and stung my eyes. The sound of water gushing through the wreckage was relentless, like a waterfall cascading down a hill. The scene was a sensory overload—an assault of sights, sounds, smells, and feelings. My mind is a tumult of thoughts, too overwhelming to process. I wanted to rewind time, to undo the chaos. It felt as though a giant spotlight was trained on us. A reporter thrust a microphone in our faces, asking for comments… but I couldn't string any words together. Nothing made sense.

Eventually, we were allowed to briefly go into the house before the fire crews left. As we stood on the doorstep, I faced my son, hands on his shoulders, our eyes locking in a deep connection and told him, *"Whatever we find inside, it's going to be okay. We're okay. All four of us."* I emphasized that anything else—everything else—was replaceable, though later I would fully grasp the extent of our loss. In that moment, it was clear what truly mattered: family. We would get through this together.

Under the eerie glow of a flashlight, with the darkness and lack of power adding to the disorientation, we navigated through debris and broken glass. The devastation was shocking: one end of the house was virtually gone, the other was nothing but a charred, blackened ruin. Fittings dripping from the walls and ceiling in meted sculptures that didn't used to be there. The sight was both surreal and chilling.

In the midst of the wreckage, a glimmer of hope emerged: the kids' rooms downstairs had escaped major damage. It was a huge blessing. They each packed a bag with some clothes, their favourite cuddly toys, and their pillows. At least they had something familiar to cling to as we faced this upheaval.

Upstairs, however, was a different story. Our bedroom, along with the kitchen, dining room and lounge had been suffocated by smoke and rendered beyond repair. The spare room and my office – was no longer there. The scale of the destruction was staggering, each room a haunting reminder of what had been lost. The anguish deepened as I feared the worst for the cats, hoping I wouldn't find their lifeless bodies amidst the wreckage. I felt a profound numbness, struggling to grasp the full extent of the loss. Everything we had worked so hard to build had vanished in an instant, and the weight of it all was crushing.

When the fire crew asked if we had somewhere to go, the answer was no. With no family in New Zealand, we felt utterly alone and vulnerable. Desperate, I called a friend, hoping we could stay at her place. She was out, but her husband agreed immediately, though he later admitted he had no idea what was happening when he hung up. I must have been incoherent, as he couldn't understand why I asked to stay in the lounge instead of their spare bedroom. Despite the confusion, we had a roof over our heads, and we were immensely grateful.

For a week, we were embraced by that generous family—held, loved, listened to, fed, and cared for—until we found a rental property and began the long journey of rebuilding our lives. Having a place to belong and people to lean on made all the difference. The comfort of a simple cup of tea with friends offered much-needed relief amidst the turmoil. Miraculously, the next day, the cats returned safe and well, a small but significant beacon of hope in our time of distress.

So many details of that night remain hazy, with questions surrounding the memories of it lingering for months. Although I'm not naturally optimistic, I chose to focus on our blessings to avoid sinking into despair. The fire crews were amazing, our neighbour—whom we barely knew—was the ideal picture of community spirit, and our friends opened their home and hearts to us. Even in the darkest moments, both literally and metaphorically, there was much to be thankful for. We were all safe, the cats were okay, and our task now was to forge a new path forward.

Some surprising observations:

- **Panic Can Escalate Crisis:** amid the fire's chaos, I was struck by a disturbing sight: a car trapped on the street, its occupants angry they couldn't move. Despite the visible emergency, their anger towards the fire crews and us only added to the turmoil. It was a stark reminder of how panic and agitation can exacerbate a crisis, and how their needs obliterated our obvious difficult situation. It was a stark reminder of the importance of maintaining calm and supporting those who are trying to manage the situation, even when it is an inconvenience to us.
- **Autopilot and Emotional Impact:** The next morning, teaching a research lecture in the same smoke-scented clothes from the day before, a colleague asked why I was there. I simply replied, "*I have nowhere else to go.*" In that moment, the reality of our situation hit me with full force. Tears streamed down my cheeks, and I allowed myself to fully experience the emotional impact for the first time, crucial to confronting and processing the crisis.
- **What You Focus on Can Shift Your Perspective:** In a critical moment, I subconsciously chose to shift my focus to my kids wellbeing. Prioritizing their emotional needs, helped us focus on what was important and stabilised our own panic and stress, which in turn helped us cope better.

- **Gaps in Knowledge Are Revealed in Crisis:** Setting up a new home from scratch exposed our lack of preparedness. When I was asked if I had any questions, I had no idea, so I asked my insurer, *"If you were in my position, knowing all you know, what would you ask yourself?"* The fact that I didn't know what questions to ask highlighted our unfamiliarity with situations like this. Thankfully, support from insurers, assessors, and builders proved invaluable, emphasizing the importance of seeking expertise and guidance in navigating unfamiliar terrain.

Writing the Next Chapter: Rising from the Ashes

How do you come back from something as devastating as this? I had never faced such profound loss. What story would I write as I moved forward?

I chose the metaphor of the Phoenix—a mythical bird that rises from its ashes—as a symbol for our journey. It felt fitting. I created a Phoenix Gratitude Journal on Facebook to share our story, keep friends and family informed, and set an intention to find something positive each day. This practice was meant to guide us through our trials until we could finally see the Phoenix rise, symbolizing our return to normalcy. Little did I know how transformative this process would become.

On some days, gratitude came easily. I could celebrate milestones like appointing a builder, clearing the last of the debris, or securing generous insurance support. These moments felt like stepping stones on our path to rebuilding both our home and our lives. They lifted my spirits and made the recovery seem possible.

But on other days, it was a struggle. I understood the importance of discipline and consistency, especially when motivation waned. My sarcasm sometimes surfaced in posts like, "*I'm really grateful today that at least the builder showed up.*" It was honest and raw, a reflection of the frustration I felt when progress seemed agonizingly slow. Yet, even on those tough days, gratitude offered a broader perspective and prevented me from spiralling into negativity. It helped me maintain a level ground amid the chaos.

Reality was far from smooth. We faced unexpected complications with the rebuild, which meant re-contracting and additional delays. Our rental funds were finite, and the pressure to move back into our home before those funds ran out was constant. Despite these hurdles, our home—our view—was worth every challenge. We focused on the finish line and pressed on with determination.

The day we moved back in was a joyous celebration. It marked a milestone, a moment of triumph. I shared a photo on my Phoenix Gratitude page of a Phoenix taking flight, symbolizing our own rise from the ashes. We were home, and we had made it through, though the journey of healing and rebuilding was far from over.

Reflecting on our experience, I wonder what you might be struggling with? How could a daily gratitude practice help you shift your focus and craft a story that leads to a more positive journey and a meaningful ending?

Reflecting Back

A house fire is more than just a catastrophic event; it's a profound upheaval that shakes you to your core. Your home is an extension of yourself, and the devastation penetrates deep into your sense of security and belonging. It's a stark reminder of the fragility of what we hold dear.

Through this harrowing experience, we discovered much about our resilience and capacity for growth in the face of overwhelming uncertainty. We were tested in ways we could never have anticipated.

I learned firsthand the power of the tools I teach: breathing, gratitude, havening, IDT, Heartmath, polyvagal and methods for regulating the nervous system. Staying connected with myself and others, maintaining a clear vision of our goals, and holding on to hopeful optimism proved indispensable. This real-life trial highlighted the profound effectiveness of these tools in even the most challenging circumstances.

One crucial lesson was the importance of documenting everything. Photographing every room, cupboard, and valuable item annually became a glaring need after the fire. In the midst of stress and chaos, our memory fails us, and having a visual record can be invaluable when details slip away.

The experience also underscored the immense value of having others hold space for you. The love, support, and presence of those who simply stood by us, without needing to solve anything, were profoundly comforting. This kindness became a treasure, a reminder of the power we all hold to uplift others.

Material possessions, I realized, are not as crucial as we often believe. The loss was significant, but finding a few precious photo albums and a surviving wooden nativity scene amidst the rubble was a poignant reminder of what truly matters. Digital backups of irreplaceable memories would have been a prudent safeguard.

I discovered strengths within myself that I hadn't known existed. My family's well-being took precedence over my career, and focusing on their needs allowed me to navigate the challenges more effectively. It revealed a depth of selflessness and resilience I hadn't previously recognized.

The rapid shift in others' responses was another eye-opener. A year after the fire, it became clear that while the trauma had faded from the forefront of people's minds, the journey of recovery was still ongoing for us. This highlighted the importance of offering ongoing support and empathy to others long after the immediate crisis has passed.

The generosity of strangers was profoundly moving. Two local restaurants, each with their own stories of hardship, gifted us meals as a gesture of kindness. Their acts of paying it forward illuminated the powerful ripples of compassion and community support.

I discovered the profound impact of holding space for my clients with even greater effectiveness. The unique nature of trauma, challenges, and loss illuminated the immense value of connection that transcends mere tools and techniques. The true power lies in simply 'being' with someone—making them feel genuinely seen, heard, and understood, no matter what they are experiencing. This realization has deepened my coaching practice, slowing my approach to allow for a richer, more attentive presence. My ability to engage fully—heart, mind, body, and soul—has grown exponentially, enhancing my capacity to support and guide clients through their own journeys with greater empathy and connection.

Finally, my faith was tested and strengthened in ways I hadn't anticipated. What I once viewed as a theoretical concept became a living, breathing part of my being. This ordeal deepened my understanding of the interconnectedness of 'we' over 'I' and reinforced the vital role of community in our health and well-being.

Each lesson learned from this ordeal has reshaped my perspective and enriched my approach to life and work.

Giving Back

Life has a way of throwing unexpected challenges our way, often when we least expect it. The fire taught me that we are all far stronger and more resilient than we could ever imagine. It also highlighted the priceless value of support during times of crisis. Some people have a strong network of people around them, others feel more alone, and there is one undeniable truth: having someone to walk beside you can make all the difference.

A coach can be that guide—someone independent to truly listen and to hear your story, witness your struggles, share tools and techniques and hold space for you as you navigate your path to healing in a way that is unique and perfect for you.

Learning to navigate through and beyond the fire taught me so much about myself, my coaching and how to support people in a crisis. I have been coaching for over 20 years, and now I am privileged to be able to offer exceptional support for people going through their own trauma. Whether that is seemingly small events which cause stress and confusion, to significant life changing moments where you are not sure how to get through. As a neuroscience-based coach, I work with people in an integrated, embodied and systemic way, drawing on all the wisdom and intelligences within and around us. Recognising that each person possesses a unique neurological fingerprint, along with their own beliefs, values, and experiences. I'm here to support you as you lovingly reconnect with your inner self, embrace your strengths, navigate life's challenges, and to guide you towards a place of wholeness and healing. I provide the level of exceptional support I know I needed and struggled to find. My experience has transformed my coaching approach to ensure a unique and authentic approach that puts you and your needs front and centre ensuring you get back on track.

As you reflect on your life and those you cherish, you might like to ask yourself:

- *How can I offer support to those around me?*
- *How can I show up even more powerfully and express love with greater clarity?*
- *What is truly precious to me, and how can I keep it safe?*
- *If today was my last day, how would I want to be? And what would I want to ensure happened?*

Be deliberate in how you engage with the world, even when it feels like everything is crumbling around you. Your presence, your care, and your intention can create ripples of change and resilience.

If you're interested in exploring how I can support you, or if you're curious about the training I provide for other coaches and individuals seeking to offer this kind of support, please reach out to me.

You can connect with me across my social media through:

Linktree: www.linktr.ee/drsuzannehenwood

If my story resonates with you, I invite you to purchase **The Ultimate Gratitude Journal**, which shares the process I used (available at many online bookstores) and you can find out more about that book here: **www.theluminosityproject.nz/the-ultimate-gratitude-journal**

And reach out if I can help you with one-on-one coaching to help you through difficult times.

CHAPTER 4

By Erica Mackay

From "should" to "choose": the power of language in life and business

My name is Erica Mackay and 10 years ago a really small incident caused me to rethink both my personal and business life completely. Missing the bus on the way to work resulted in me revisiting the major decisions in my life, trying to find a pattern. The pattern that I found was difficult to ignore. Every time I had followed the advice of the "should" I ended up unhappy, stressed and overwhelmed.

The word "should" is often criticised in discussions about mental health because it carries implicit expectations and judgments that can exacerbate feelings of inadequacy, guilt, and anxiety. That definitely was the case with me.

As I share my story, I encourage you to think about your own cases of following the "should." Did it serve you well or cause you stress?

What the country needed

I was born in a small town in South Africa to two loving parents. I was born in the apartheid era, which, for those of you don't know, was when it was a racist regime and my family and I were on the wrong side of the race card. I don't really remember being affected by apartheid until I started school. My earliest memory was that we lived in a township called Bronville, and that's where all the brown people like me had to live, but the schooling in the area was really non-existent. The teachers often didn't pitch up and when they did get to school, they were often drunk. The school was broken into often, there were no textbooks and as a result the pass rate was really low.

My father was a firm believer in education, and so he persuaded a local headmaster to accept me into white school. This was a headmaster that went to the same church as my dad, and he convinced this headmaster that I needed a good education. I was really the first non-white person in a white school in this little town where we lived in. Half the pupils in that school were taken out by their parents, and half of them remained. The school really took a knock, but the teachers and the headmaster stood up for me.

In hindsight this put a lot of pressure on me as a small child, thinking I needed to be perfect. I needed to stand up for all brown people, because if I didn't get brilliant grades, if I didn't do really well, if I wasn't really nice, if I said anything that would offend anyone, it would be a sign to all those who left the school that they were right, that it was a big mistake to take this brown girl into the school. That life lesson stayed with me for most of my life and held me back in a lot of ways, because it meant I was always striving for perfectionism. I was always scared to stand out from the crowd. Didn't want to speak my mind, in case it offended people. I did what I thought I should do what I should do to please everyone.

The word "should" suggests a predetermined standard or expectation that one is expected to meet. These expectations can feel overwhelming or unattainable. For example, statements like "I should be happy," "I should be more productive," or "I should not feel this way" set a benchmark that may not be realistically achievable. This creates a disconnect between where a person is and where they believe they "should" be, fostering feelings of failure or inadequacy.

What society needed

The second area of my life that was full of "shoulds" is my culture. I come from quite a male dominated, masculine culture where the woman's role is to have babies and look after the family. My mother was primarily a full time stay at home mum and my dad was the main financial contributor which was the accepted norm at that time. In the township where we lived it went even further. Girls were encouraged to get married as soon as possible. You were encouraged to get a guy to marry you by any means possible, and that often meant getting pregnant. If you finished high school without having a husband, the general feeling was that you must be ugly. If you went further and got a university degree, which was unheard of where in where I lived, you must be hideous. No man will ever touch you.

The pressure of what I should be doing surrounded me, but my mind was rebelling. I wanted to be educated. My father wanted us to be educated. I didn't want to get pregnant. Despite this I got engaged at age 16 to a guy who was twice my age. In our township he was considered a good catch and I was told by most people how lucky I was. My parents didn’t like him though. By the time we got engaged he already had four children from four different women, but they'd all been girls, and so he hadn't married them because he wanted a boy. I was just next in line. I didn’t see it though.

Luckily, I had some internal rules. We had a long engagement because I wanted to finish school first and then go to university. It was during that whole period, and actually the day before our wedding, when I caught him cheating. I found out that he'd been cheating all through our engagement. I broke off the engagement and left, although all our friends told me that I was making a mistake. “That’s just the way men are.” And “You are so lucky that he wants you.” I moved to another city to attend university and threw myself into my career but eventually the societal pressure came back. So I did the "right thing". I got married at age 30 and had 2 children, rather late in life according to cultural norms. I love my family, and I can't imagine my life without them. I also love my career and travelling the world and if I hadn't had the pressure, I don't know what road my life would have taken.

Another area where I was affected by "shoulds" was when I went to university. Back then you needed to be either a doctor or an accountant if you wanted to be successful. I am quite squeamish and so I chose accountancy. I really hated it. I failed my first year at university and then I had a vacation job at an accountancy firm, where I finally realised the truth. I was not cut out to be an accountant. I changed my degree to marketing and ended up in a career I love.

Growing up, we get told we should do things. The word "should" is frequently rooted in societal, familial, or cultural expectations rather than your personal authentic feelings or needs. This can lead you to prioritise external validation over internal well-being. This external pressure can lead to feeling overwhelmed and making decisions which are contrary to what you actually want.

What womanhood needed

There are so many different messages we are exposed to as women, and I have spent most of my life trying to live up to those expectations. I have already shared the societal pressure of being a wife and a mother, but there is also pressure to have a career. Women have been fighting for years for the right to work, to vote and to have a voice. I threw myself into that dream and worked really hard to become a successful career woman. Outwardly I was seen as successful. Inwardly it took a toll.

At the peak of my corporate career, I was a Marketing Director for an International company. I looked after 16 different countries and managed over 300 people. I got to travel all over the world and meet amazing people. On the other hand, my health was suffering as I ate too much junk food and drank lots of energy drinks and coffee. I didn't have any time for exercise and my excessive smoking and alcohol consumption did nothing to help. It's also a sad fact of the corporate world that you sometimes have to work with people who you are just not aligned with and that just adds to the corporate stress.

It took a long time for me to accept that there is more than one definition of success, and many ways to still stand tall and proud as a woman. I finally decided to quit the corporate world. I'm now an entrepreneur. which means I get to choose who I work with and for. It's people who I resonate with, those with similar values to mine. I choose my hours, which means I'm there for the kids if they need me. I can take an afternoon off if one of my kids are ill. I still consider myself successful, and more importantly, I'm happy.

Sometimes the "shoulds" are subtle and you don't notice it until after the fact. Someone I really respect and admire, heard me speak once and really felt that I would succeed as a public speaker. For a while I was swept along in the glamour and his excitement and enthusiasm, but I became more and more uncomfortable. Once I stopped to reflect, I realised that

I was trying to live his vision for me and not my dream for myself. I didn't want to disappoint him and so I kept going but actually I wasn't having any fun. I don't mind public speaking but it's not what I want to do as a full-time career. Now I do occasional keynote speeches as part of my bigger offering and that's enough for me.

"Should" language often reflects a fixed mindset, implying that there is a correct way of feeling, thinking, or behaving that one must adhere to. This can limit our ability to accept and adapt to our experiences. Adopting a more flexible, growth-oriented mindset can be far more beneficial. Instead of thinking "I should not be feeling anxious," a more helpful approach might be "I notice I am feeling anxious, and that's okay. What can I do to care for myself in this moment?"

What my family needed

When I looked back at my life following the missed bus incident, I realised what I'd done is to be a good wife and a good mum, as defined by society and the media. I had given up most of my friends. I'd stopped doing any of the stuff I loved. When I wasn't at work, I was spending all my time doing what a good wife and mom should do, as told me, by society or my family or culturally, and therefore there was very little joy left in my life other than my kids and my husband.

I had really limited time with my children because I was travelling for work so much. Even when I was at home, I saw them for a few minutes in the morning as I dropped them off at breakfast club. In the evenings they were often asleep by the time I got home. I compensated for my mum-guilt by buying them toys and games and sweets after every trip. On weekends they got all my attention with trips and outings and really anything they wanted. I was totally responsible for all the cooking, laundry and cleaning in the house and would wake up extra early to get it all done. There was no place for me or what I needed.

I started to make time for myself by asking for help and sharing the responsibilities with my family. I started going to live music again with friends, because I love live music. I started playing the saxophone again because I'd stopped doing that. I slowly started making time to do things I loved, not every day, but enough to make me happy. I started reconnecting with friends and getting out into nature more.

I really looked at making sure that there's less of "I should" and more of "I could", and by changing the conversation, things became a pleasure instead of a chore. I still do all the cooking, but now I love cooking. I'm not doing it because it's a chore and I have to do it. I'm doing it because I love cooking. Now and again, when I don't have time or I'm going to be late, I delegate the cooking to my kids or my husband. And they actually enjoy my food more, once they understand the work that goes into preparing a meal.

"Should" statements are often self-critical, reinforcing negative self-talk. For instance, someone might think, "I should be able to handle this better," which can lead to a spiral of self-blame and shame when they inevitably struggle. This kind of self-criticism can deepen mental health struggles by reinforcing a narrative of personal failure or lack of worth.

The use of "should" also often creates a gap between your current reality and an idealised version of what you think your reality "ought" to be. This dissonance can increase distress because it focuses on the difference between where a person is and where you believe you should be. Instead of accepting our current feelings and working through them, we are caught in a loop of trying to reconcile this gap, which can prevent healing and growth.

What I needed

The missing-the-bus incident happened when I have just turned 40. There were a few pressures happening at that time and missing the bus was the tipping point. The day after my birthday I received a letter from the NHS congratulating me on entering a new age bracket. I was now in the same age bracket as my mum and although I know that the new health checks that they wanted me to go on were meant for my own well-being, it felt like turning 40 was the beginning of the end.

I was living in London at the time, and one day I was running for bus, and even though the bus driver saw me coming, he carried on driving. It was not a big deal because in London there's a bus every 10 minutes. Suddenly the bus stopped in the middle of the road and this young blonde girl walked across the road and got on the bus. I was so angry about the unfairness of the situation. I spent the whole week and the following weekend stewing about this event and thinking about the fact that I was 40 and my life was empty and without much joy.

My entire being was rebelling against this. I didn't want to be joyless and exhausted and stressed all the time. I replayed all the major decisions in my life and came to the realisation that I needed to focus on what I chose to do rather than what others told me I "should" be doing. the word "should" can be a harmful trigger that perpetuates negative feelings, reinforces a judgmental mindset, and hinders recovery by promoting unrealistic expectations and self-criticism. Moving away from "should" and adopting language that is more accepting, flexible, and compassionate can help support mental health recovery by fostering self-acceptance, promoting self-care, and encouraging a growth mindset.

Now I can identify "should" messages as they arrive and take a step back to question their validity. Who decided that? Does it apply to me? Does that message bring me joy or make me uncomfortable. I still make mistakes and end up down the wrong path but that's the beauty of life. We can always change direction and do what we choose to do.

Conclusion

"Should" undermines your authenticity by implying that there is a right or wrong way to feel or behave, and this can diminish our ability to make choices that are best for our own mental health. It suggests a moral imperative, which can be disempowering. Moreover, "should" is inherently lacking in self-compassion. It is a directive rather than a supportive statement, often leaving little room for understanding, patience, or forgiveness toward oneself.

When I work with businesses, I hear quite a lot of "shoulds", and I love helping them work through that and actually build marketing plans that will work for both their target clients and themselves. I love helping businesses find the clients that they want to work with and find the clients that want to work with them.

If I get asked "Should I be on social media?" I can help them work through the real problem which is often about finding and attracting clients. By really identifying your target audience, working out what messages would resonate with them and then looking at which channels they hang out in, we can craft a marketing plan that is comfortable to follow, and which will be successful. We also look at the activities that they would be comfortable doing. For example, not everyone is comfortable posting videos about themselves so forcing them to be active on TikTok will not be a successful long-term strategy. Eventually they will hate doing it so much that they stop. I don't believe in putting so much energy into something you don't enjoy when the same amount of energy into something enjoyable will lead to better long-term results.

T.S Eliot said, "Only those who will risk going too far can possibly find out how far one can go." Having the courage to question all the "should" messages in our lives will take us to places we haven't yet dreamed of, but it will ultimately allow us to be happy. Everyone has their own definition of success and happiness and once you find yours, decisions will become much easier to make.

Erica Mackay, Marketing Detective

The Marketing Detective Agency

www.themarketingdetectiveagency.com

https://www.linkedin.com/in/erica-mackay/

COURAGE

"THE PRIVILEGE OF A LIFETIME IS BEING WHO YOU ARE."

– JOSEPH CAMPBELL

CHAPTER 5

Defying the Odds: Turning 'You Can't' Into 'Watch Me'

By Zoe Plumley

The Power of Mindset

Mindset is an incredible thing. It shapes you as a person; it creates your coping mechanisms and depending on your mindset will cause positive or negative opportunities in life. I remember being so proud of telling my family that I wanted to be a doctor. I wanted to help people and to make a difference and I was told no - you can't do that. That is my first memory of someone telling me that 'I can't', sadly however it was definitely not the last.

How you face adversity totally depends on your mindset. I have always tried to look at life in a positive way; no matter what is going on in your life, there is always someone in a worse situation. Sometimes you just need to look a little bit harder than others to find the silver lining.

So who am I who allegedly has known the sharp end of the knife of life? Who am I to think that what I have to say will make any difference? Who am I to inspire anyone? The answer to this is that I am an incredible human being, an incredible mum, incredible partner and a darn good business owner and I care about people.

At the age of 15 I was involved in an accident at school which caused me to be temporarily paralysed and in a wheelchair with an uncertain prognosis. I could have given up, but I refused to allow my emotions to rule me. I put my stubbornness to good use and on my 18th birthday I walked for the first time unaided.

After evaluating all my options and with the words 'You can't be a doctor' in my head, I settled on going into a different health care profession - the field of nursing and I absolutely loved it! For over a decade I worked in various sectors from secure mental health hospitals, prisons, high care units and A&E. I loved the variety of the work and more than that I loved making that difference, knowing that I'd helped someone, even if sometimes it was just to make them a cup of tea if they were afraid, or to hold their hand so that they knew they weren't by themselves when they passed away.

However, throughout all of this I had one continuous barrier to doing what I loved most - my health. I would every three months (you could time it) be admitted to the high care unit with an asthma attack, or with my heart condition, which I later had cardiac surgery for. It got to the point where as brilliant as the NHS was for looking after their patients, they could only follow the tick box employee sickness process and I had to make a choice; leave of my own choosing, or be told to leave.

Life's Curveballs

This massive life change caused me to fall into the unknown. Link this with an unexpected move from England to Wales to go into a women's aid refuge with my then 3-year-old son and life was scary and stressful. It felt like I had no control and could only go in the direction that others were suggesting.

Eventually life stabilised. I found myself a new job working in recruitment, compliance and safeguarding and although my health still gave me a few blips, for the most part things were settled. This was until the dreaded word "redundancy" echoed through the halls.

I remember climbing up the stairs with my team, up to the conference room and we met the HR team coming down the stairs in tears. We knew then that the echo was real and a couple of minutes later it was confirmed.

I felt numb. I'd never been made redundant before, that comfort and security of knowing I had a job, knowing that I could provide for my family had gone with just that one word. We were told that the redundancies would start to happen within the next couple of months. However as I hadn't been there long enough to be able to get any redundancy pay, I went into hyperfocus. I needed to find a new job quickly.

Eventually I did find a new job and although it meant a longer commute, it was purely a recruitment role and that meant it was my first ever 9-5, Monday-Friday job and that sounded like heaven to me.

It wasn't an easy start to the role. Some people were welcoming, others took longer to get to know, but I enjoyed the work and was determined to make myself a success in the company. Six weeks into my probationary period I took that test that only females can take and low and behold a little plus sign appeared. I had tried for years with my ex-husband to fall pregnant. I had been told I couldn't have any more children, and yet here I was, pregnant with an amazing partner, but in a brand new job. I think everyone would agree that this was less than ideal.

I kept this secret from work for a couple of weeks (mainly because I was trying to process and trying to get a midwife appointment was a challenge), but then the day came where I had to ask for leave to attend my first midwife appointment. I told my line manager and put the leave request form on the managing director's desk. An hour later I was called into the office and told I was being fired and put on gardening leave immediately. To say that I was blindsided was an understatement. I had not had any complaints or issues raised to me. In fact I had been told I was settling in and doing well and this just completely broke me.

I remember calling the GP surgery hysterically. The poor receptionist that answered was just amazing. I don't know quite how much she understood between my sobs, but she knew that I needed help and she told me to come straight in and see a GP as an emergency appointment. I may not know which receptionist she was (I'm part of a massive GP Practice), but I will forever be grateful to her.

I already had a diagnosis of depression, anxiety and PTSD from my domestic abuse, and this had just spiralled me into a further state of depression. I felt completely lost, worthless, scared - I literally just didn't know what to do. Two jobs lost in a matter of months and neither from a situation I had ever experienced before. The firing especially left a really sick feeling in my stomach as I always strive to be the best of the best and although I am sure it was an unfair firing, it still made me feel as if I deserved to be in a rubbish dump.

The GP signed me off with depression for a couple of months and said to come back if I needed more time. Again I couldn't fault her - she was amazing, empathetic and genuinely couldn't do enough for me.

Covid and a New Reality

A month later came that BBC television broadcast by the then Prime Minister Boris Johnson. It was 2020, Covid had become a pandemic and we, as a country were being put into a mandatory lockdown. I remember sitting there watching him talk with my partner on one side and son on the other and just thinking this can't be real. I remember seeing photos of the Chinese with their face masks on all the time and thinking I'm so glad I don't live there, and yet here we were, with mandatory facemasks, mandatory stay at home orders and a panic buy on toilet roll and pasta.

For me, I lived in a little bubble during this time. I was on the shielding list so literally wasn't allowed to go anywhere except medical appointments as the risk to me was so high. If I caught Covid, the thoughts were I wouldn't survive it. I remember being so grateful that I was pregnant. I was a high-risk pregnancy due to all my other health conditions. I had to be seen weekly in the clinic and that gave me human interaction. I dubbed it my social life and I enjoyed it.

What I didn't enjoy were the times when the community midwives would send me to the hospital because they couldn't find a heartbeat and when the sonographer would send me back to see the consultant after a scan because they wanted me reviewed and this had to happen alone. Covid law prevented me from having George with me at any point. He wasn't allowed at any appointment, or at any scan - he was completely detached from the whole experience and this was difficult for the both of us.

On the 9th of October 2020 my daughter was born via c-section and although planned there were complications and I ended up being rushed back into surgery a few hours later. George was allowed with me when I was on the labour ward only. He wasn't allowed to spend more than a few hours with me and our newborn daughter. Due to my post op complications we spent 4 days on the postnatal ward and all I could do was facetime my George and my son Logan so that they could see us. This was not the precious bonding time that as a family we craved.

Still, I came home and life as a family of four began. We remained in lockdown with homeschooling still being dictated by the government. I genuinely thanked myself for going down the health care route and not the teacher career route, as I take my hat off to all teachers - I do not have the patience!

When Larna was just 2 months old I literally turned to stone and this is no dramatisation. My health gave me a new present on Christmas Day. I had always suffered with joint pain and a couple of days before Christmas we were out walking looking at the Christmas lights and I couldn't put any weight through my wrists to push the pram up and down the curb. I made the flippant comment of 'The cold must have got into my bones'. However my life was literally about to be turned upside down. On Christmas Day I awoke to severe pain in every single joint of my body. It was all I could do to not cry. I wasn't able to open my presents or help my children open theirs. I couldn't even pop a paracetamol out of its packet, and it was definitely the most painful shower of my life. As Christmas Day went on I physically blew up in front of my family. The swelling was unreal and the more I swelled, the more painful it all became. We ended up leaving my family gathering early because I just didn't know what to do with myself and on the way home I felt like I couldn't breathe. I couldn't expand my lungs enough because of the pain.

When we got home George put the kids to bed and I called the out of hours GP service who immediately dispatched an ambulance. This was my first experience of emergency services during Covid. One paramedic was absolutely amazing, but the other you could tell was deeply traumatised by the pandemic and was presenting as almost paranoid that I had Covid, even though I had tested negative. At this point I turned to stone. I couldn't even lie down on the stretcher, move any of my limbs and if you brushed against me I would scream with pain. The A&E team basically wrote me off because I had pneumonia (which I was already being treated for). They said that muscle aches and pains are to be expected. Consequently they gave me a dose of oramorph and sent me on my way. I couldn't even move my arms enough to put my coat on so was expected just to leave A&E in December without a coat when I was already unwell. I have had pneumonia at least once a year since I was 17 - this was not muscle aches and pains from that!

For the next couple of weeks I would speak to the GP or out of hours daily. They gave me steroids and strong painkillers, but nothing really worked. It got to the point that one night I was stuck on my living room floor and couldn't move to get to the bathroom - I was 32 and had wet myself. I was humiliated. I was referred to rheumatology. The consultant asked me about my symptoms and how it was affecting me. I asked him if he'd ever had to change a baby's nappy without using his thumbs? It's impossible and yet that was the situation I was in. They sent me for tests and scans and then the diagnosis came, 'You have Rheumatoid Arthritis (RA)'. I was then put onto medication which suppressed my immune system, which is an issue when you already suffer with regular chest infections, and lots of other life changing medications such as biologic therapies. However, it was what I needed to do if I wanted any chance of being able to move and be a mum.

At the same time as I was going through my diagnosis for RA there was another battle on the home front. George had contracted Covid from the care home he was working at and he was incredibly sick. I vividly remember speaking to an out of hours doctor as George's oxygen level was 88% and being told not to attend the hospital as there were no beds, but I should call back if he gets worse. To know that your loved one was critically ill with a disease that had caused hundreds of thousands of deaths worldwide was bad enough, but to find that help wasn't available whilst battling a disease myself that limited my mobility and looking after two children was probably the hardest time of my life. George went on to develop Long Covid and multiple other diagnoses. Overnight we went from George being my carer to me being his.

Making a Change

This was the pivotal time where I had to make a decision about how mine and my family's lives were going to be. In less than a year we had gone from a solid 2 income family, to relying purely on statutory maternity and sickness benefits - this wasn't sustainable. I also knew that I didn't want to ever be put in the situation where I could lose my job again. I wanted control and security of knowing that I would always know I had a job. Historically I had owned a childcare agency and a printing business so I knew I was good at business - I knew that I could do it again, but what?

I took a long hard think about my life, my values, what I enjoyed doing and what I missed. It came to me that I missed helping people - I missed making a difference. So I retrained. I became accredited in Coaching, NLP (neuro linguistic programming) and Timeline Therapy. My coaching business and journey was launched. I coach business owners with health conditions, disabilities and neurodiversity in disability impact and coping strategies. It works because I can empathise - I have literally walked in their shoes and know how they're feeling and have experienced the same barriers.

A couple of months into my coaching journey it got flagged to me by one of my coaching peers that she was aware I was also doing some admin for my clients. To me this was just me helping them out - they were overwhelmed with it or didn't know what to do and my purpose was to help, so of course I offered to take it off their hands. What I didn't know was that this was actually a whole other job role and after being sent to help out a Virtual Assistant who needed an extra pair of hands as their associate, I realised that I had been doing two jobs, to quote a supermarket shop - "two for the price of one".

I then expanded my coaching firm to include virtual assistant services and my whole world exploded. I was busier than I could ever have imagined - to the point that I needed to take on associate virtual assistants and coaches just to be able to keep up with demand. I felt fulfilled - I couldn't help everyone, but I knew that between me and my team we'd give it our absolute best.

Building a Thriving Business

Nowadays my coaching company still offers disability impact and coping strategies coaching, but we can also offer other coaching services such as standard business coaching. We offer 1:1 sessions, group sessions, have an amazing membership and have an ever growing community of business owners who have faced health challenges but, like me, have the mindset of 'You say I can't - you just watch me'.

My virtual assistant company has gone from strength to strength. I now have a team of 12 (not bad for a little lady on top of a mountain in a little Welsh village) and we can offer support in everything from general admin, tech support, social media, bookkeeping, transcription and so much more. One of the people I know refers to me as an 'admin pick n mix sweet shop' which I think is brilliant!

I'm also so proud to say that we specialise in helping people with their UK disability benefit forms (PIP, DLA, ESA etc) and currently have a 100% success rate on this. We also support Blue Badge applications, and the fantastic UK government grant called Access 2 Work which is a brilliant scheme for people with health conditions that are either employed, self employed or looking to start a business within the next six weeks. With Access 2 Work you can get access to coaching, support workers, equipment, software and so much more - it is absolutely life changing.

Personally, I am a champion for Disability Inclusion. I am a keynote speaker on this, an advocate and am passionate about making a change. I want to be the support that I so badly needed, but was missing.

Never forget that just because we have a health condition or disability does not mean that we can't do things. It just means that we might need to take a longer route, but we'll get there and we'll be proud of doing what people said we couldn't.

Facebook: www.facebook.com/groups/1961920684174222

Wellness Tracker: www.subscribepage.io/wellness-tracker

Time Tracker: www.subscribepage.io/time-tracker

LinkedIn: www.linkedin.com/in/zoeplumley

L&L Virtual Assistant Services Facebook:

www.facebook.com/profile.php?id=100094621924739

L&L Coaching Services Facebook:

www.facebook.com/profile.php?id=61558179575368

L&L Virtual Assistant Services Instagram:

www.instagram.com/landlvaservices

Website: www.landlvaservices.co.uk

Website: www.landlcoachingservices.co.uk

CHAPTER 6

By Kelly Watts

From Darkness to Dreams – How I overcame the grey cloud

I just can't. I remember those words well. It had a hold on my life for a few years when I was in my late twenties. At what I thought was the prime time of my life (looking back now I know this thought was naive!) I felt like it was all swept away from me in a heartbeat.

This period of my life was from a trigger of events, it started with a long-term relationship break-up, to losing my nan and everything that happened in between and after these two big events. Do you know the saying it doesn't rain it pours, well this was how this period of my life felt for me. I was grieving the life that I thought was going to be my happy ever after.

After this break up, I was now alone, living on my own and just had my two dogs to keep me going. This is when it all started going dark and grey. Walking around with a dark cloud constantly above my head. You know the cartoon when you see someone walking around with a grey cloud above their head pouring with rain, following them everywhere. And they are just staring down at the floor. You can see the weight of the world on their shoulders. Well, that was my reality. And that's when those words started in my head. Whenever I wanted to do anything, even just a basic need for myself like cook a meal. 'I just can't'. Not because I didn't want to. I just couldn't.

I was depressed as fuck, to put it lightly. And not just depressed, I had crippling anxiety to go with it too. And I couldn't tell you which one was worse, so imagine having both at the same time. Yet I am here today. Me. Collaborating with 27 other incredible authors, sharing my story of darkness, the road to entrepreneurship and living my dreams. I am still pinching myself thinking about this!

One of the most impactful sayings I have heard is from Henry Ford - "Whether you think you can or think you can't, you're right". I begin my story with how these words were the ruler of me. And unfortunately, at this time, these words were not due to limiting beliefs.

Down the rabbit hole

Have you ever experienced so much loss in one go, one event after the other it led you down a rabbit hole to the darkest place in your life? It's like a snowball effect. One thing happens. Then another. And another. Until you're in this giant snowball that just keeps on spiralling until you can't go any further.

But you can't feel yourself going down. It's only when you're at rock bottom you realise how low you actually are. That feeling at rock bottom is like no other. Every little thing you need to do feels like the biggest effort in the world. When you are depressed, life becomes overwhelming. I remember when I was at my lowest point of going through a period where I had to wear my work clothes to bed ready for the morning, because it was such a struggle to get dressed each day. Dressing for most of us is just getting up and getting dressed. But when you're depressed it's not that. It's broken down into so many different tasks. It's underwear, that's knickers, bra, socks. Then top and trousers and a jumper or jacket. Then shoes. It's not just one task, it's around 7 or 8 tasks and it was so difficult to do every day. I also couldn't brush my teeth in the evening as this was just another task to do. There's such a whole host of feelings and emotions when you're really depressed and anxious, it's hard to give you the full extent of day-to-day life living with it.

Any ounce of motivation I had to act on there and then, because if I didn't the moment would go, and I couldn't bring myself to do it later. I went through two rounds of depression and anxiety. To be honest, I couldn't tell you whether anxiety or depression is worse, so it's hard to imagine what having them both at the same time feels like. What I just described about the struggle with getting dressed was the second round of depression, which is when I was at rock bottom.

Round one

The first time I experienced depression I didn't hit rock bottom. This experience was the first encounter I had with antidepressants. I remember going to the doctors after a few weeks following my break up as I couldn't cope. I needed time off work, time for me and time away from the world. That first set of antidepressants did not last very long! I was working in adult social services at the time, and I was fortunate to have very supportive managers and colleagues who supported my decision and encouraged me to get help for myself. I remember having four weeks off work. In that time, I tried and gave up on fluoxetine, as it completely changed my mood every 30 seconds. It was like being on a terrifying roller coaster of emotions, not knowing how you're going to be feeling one minute to the next.

During the four weeks I stayed with my mum for the first two. She lived in Peterborough and I was living in Cardiff at the time. I was just wanting to get away from my routine and have a complete break away. I remember just getting up and deciding I was going, and after some bad directions, a few wrong turns and nearly running out of petrol (this was before I had a satnav – which I bought soon after!) my mum and her partner (who had given me some dodgy directions from an airport roundabout!) ended up meeting me not far away and driving back to theirs around midnight.

I think the reason that this had hit me so hard was, up to this point, I had been quite naive in life. I was fortunate that at 27 I hadn't hit many nails in the road in life, so to have a big life event happen really knocked me for six. My grandfather had died when I was 24, and up until that point that was the only hardship I had gone through in life. And I think that is why everything hit me like a ton of bricks. I was fortunate to have had everything go well until this point. But also, unless you go through these journeys in life, how can you prepare yourself for it?

It's funny how it affects us differently. This first bout of depression I remember losing a stone in weight as I couldn't eat because of the anxiety. When I returned from staying with my mum for two weeks, I was starting to feel better because I wasn't putting on a front, having to go into work and show up for others. The last two weeks I was off I binge watched Dexter on Netflix. I was starting to feel better slowly.

After a few weeks of being home I started running. I remember getting up at 6.30am every day to go for a run, taking the dogs with me. With the weight loss and the newfound feeling slightly better because of the exercise, I noticed that I was starting to get addicted to it.

Then I was having to buy myself new clothes because I had lost weight, and I remember getting addicted to spending money. I wasn't getting into debt, but whenever I went to a supermarket, I had to buy that top, or an item of clothing. The spending didn't last long fortunately, but it was just another thing that my brain went through at the time.

What happened next

Everything was starting to look up. My best friend had moved in with me whilst she was studying at university. I was feeling a bit better about myself because I was fit and healthy, loved how I looked and enjoyed my new found running. I was 27 and felt like I was starting over again, childless with no relationship and time was catching up with me to settle down with someone. I decided I was ready to start dating again so I signed up to Plenty of Fish. Oh my god.

The relationship breakdown I talked about earlier, I had been in for 5 years. I hadn't met him – or anyone previously - on a dating site, so this was a completely new world to me. And what a world – and I don't mean for the right reasons! For someone who has always been loyal, trustworthy, honest and reliable, the online dating world was not made for me! It was like they didn't treat you like a person behind the profile. They were either after trying to get laid as much as possible, or not actually serious about having a relationship.

The first few dates I went on, I remember them saying yes, they wanted to meet up again. So, I used to get my hopes up whenever I met someone. I only used to speak to one man at a time, as I wanted to get to know one person and put my energy into that. But when you get messed around, realise they aren't serious or get ghosted as the term is now, it does eventually get you down, and there's only so much negativity you can take. I came off the site.

During this time my nan had recently fallen and broken her hip.

I can't remember exactly when, but not long after I had a phone call saying that she only had 24-48 hours to live. I was in a coffee shop with my friend and remember breaking down in tears saying I couldn't go through it all again. This was a few months after I had gone through the relationship break down. I didn't want to go through all that shit again, the depression and the battle. I couldn't. But she said to me 'yes you can, you're strong.'

I went straight to see my nan. But instead of the next 24-48 hours, she actually lived for around six more weeks. It was six weeks of finishing work, going straight to visit her at Llandough hospital, which wasn't far from where I was working down Cardiff Bay. Six weeks of seeing her every day, thinking is this the last time I am going to see her. And then it happened. I was out on a long 10k run around the bay and had the call to go straight to the hospital. It was December, a Thursday and a week before Christmas. I sat there with my family and it happened a few hours later, she died with us around her and me holding her hand.

Ten steps back

It all went downhill again for me after this. This is when I started spiralling down again. A few months before I had been to see a medium who had said to me 'be prepared, because you're going to be really low, the lowest you will have ever been.' I remember at the time shaking it off, thinking I have just been through this and there is no way I am going to get that low again.

Once you have been depressed, you recognise signs when it's popping its head again. So, when I felt this happening, I used to sit down and work out what was going well and wasn't going well, and get rid of the negative things. Because I had promised myself, I wasn't going through it again.

Our brains are amazing, but equally terrifying. Unless you have been through rock bottom, it's hard, and probably pointless, to try and put into words how it feels there. Apart from feeling numb, and just totally and utterly sad (among many other things) you feel the need to hide. I was still working in the council, but now I had changed my job and was a social work assistant (I eventually got the job on my 4th try in that period of overcoming depressive period number 1).

Working in the social care sector I was very fortunate that the colleagues, and others in surrounding teams, were caring and supportive. I had started in the council in the admin team, before working my way up through the departments to this job as a social work assistant. When I was in the throes of this depression, I used to walk into the office early, with my head down and as fast as I could to avoid making eye contact so no-one would speak to me. One morning I tried to do this, but my colleagues were obviously aware that I wasn't myself and in need of some help. I was walking through and was cornered, with big hugs and their mobile phone numbers being passed to me, all through this massive kindness and wanting to help. 'Ring me if you ever need to talk', 'if you feel you need to talk just text me'. I just remember how kind this was, and I was also obviously embarrassed that my invisibility cloak hadn't worked that day! It is hard to explain the feeling I felt at that moment that people had noticed, even though I was trying to avoid everyone. It turns out you can't avoid human kindness.

The council offered a counselling service for staff through their trained counsellors who worked in the drug and alcohol team, and so I got in contact with them as I felt I needed to talk to somebody. When you're depressed it's hard to talk to friends and family. I was very grateful for this service; they could see I needed help and I had a lot more counselling than the four sessions generally allocated for staff. They directed me to the doctors, as they could see my mental health was not in a very good place.

I returned to the doctors. I noticed I was getting quite manic in some behaviours. I was still running, but now I was using it as a form of self-harm. I was over exercising and not eating enough. The doctor put me back on antidepressants, citalopram this time. And my journey on these lasted for several years. I call it a journey, because again life isn't plain sailing when you're depressed, have anxiety and are relying on antidepressants to help you get through each day.

As time went on, and time goes very slowly when you are depressed, I was very slowly progressing and starting to feel better. But as I went one step forward, I would hit a bump in the road and it would take me ten steps back mentally. I couldn't pick off where I ended, I had to start again from those ten steps back. It just felt like a never-ending battle and that I would never feel better again. I would try to wean myself off antidepressants, but the need for them still clung there when I tried to lower the dose. I was stuck on the high dose for years due to this.

Back to the pond

For my sins, I started to go back on Plenty of Fish. I still had this yearning for something I was missing. But again, I would allow myself to get messed about, thinking I had to give everyone a chance in case they were 'the one'. I did eventually meet one person. He definitely wasn't 'the one' and he was definitely not a nice person. But because I was depressed, I couldn't see that I was more worthy than how I was treated. I unexpectedly ended up pregnant around a year later. I went through a turbulent solo pregnancy where I experienced the most horrendous morning sickness for the whole nine months, SPD and a host of other pregnancy related symptoms. After an eventful 42-hour labour, including tears and stitches, I eventually gave birth to my little boy. My Oscar. My new world. This was where life turned a corner.

I was still depressed and on antidepressants when I gave birth, but I was fortunate that it didn't decline, and I was also monitored and supported for postnatal depression. Because I was on antidepressants during the pregnancy, my son did have withdrawal symptoms from them. But this didn't last long and he was completely fine after a few days.

After a week I went home, with this little bundle of joy. When he was around eight months old, I stopped taking the antidepressants. I had been weaning myself off them, but I just stopped taking them. Guess what happened? Nothing! I was no longer reliant on them. I think what helped was just being a mum. I now had that focus on looking after someone that was completely reliant on me. Looking after just the two of us gave my life a different purpose and happiness that helped with easing the depression over time.

I do feel that Oscar saved me. It was not the journey I expected to go on, and it definitely was not planned. But I know if I hadn't had him my life would be completely different today. I brought Oscar up on my own until I moved in with my partner when Oscar turned eight. And yes - I did meet him on Plenty of fish! But this time around things were different. I valued myself, and I could spot the dickheads a mile off, so I didn't go anywhere near them. I met one of the most caring and lovely people I could, and our family of three and my happy ever after is now complete.

The power of WHY

After being a single parent for so many years, it made me think of all the things we could never do because I was always on a part-time salary. I was now working in a school as a TA, and although the hours suited us for Oscar being in school and for me being able to be home with him during half term, I knew there was more to life. I wanted to be able to give us the time and financial freedom that working for someone else would never give us. I wanted to be able to pick him up from school and not be tired after looking after other people's children all day. I wanted to be able to say yes, instead of saying no because we couldn't afford it.

So, it motivated me to look at what I could do. I knew I wouldn't get this freedom working for someone else, so I had to start looking at how I could create this new life myself.

Last year I started my coaching business. I help tired women who want to leave teaching create a coaching business by using their transferable skills to get started in coaching. There is so much tiredness and burnout for teachers, I want to help prevent them getting into this downward spiral and their mental health having an impact on them and their families. I believe that without going through the experiences I did, I would not be as resilient as I am today. I now use that as a drive, and I no longer use excuses to stop me from creating an extraordinary life.

When I was depressed the second time, I remember the doctor prescribing me a book from the library to read about depression. This opened my eyes to me seeing that what I was experiencing was an illness, and just having that education and learning about depression when I was going through it was really helpful. If you feel really low or that you are going through depression yourself, I would suggest going to a doctor, and also talking to others about what you are going through. Talk to your family or friends. Don't be on your own for long periods of time. If you know someone going through it, check in on them. They may not give much back, but you don't understand how much it means to them knowing someone is looking out for them.

I have just quit my job to focus full time on my business so I can help other mums to do the same. I had no background in business. I learned. I failed. I got back up again. I now help other mums to start their business, without all the mistakes I made.

I would not be where I am today if it wasn't for having Oscar. I am a firm believer in everything happens for a reason, even if it's not necessarily where you imagine you will be, or have to go through. Which brings me back to what I said in chapter one. One of the most impactful sayings I have heard is from Henry Ford - "Whether you think you can or think you can't, you're right".

I can. I'm doing it right now, and that's because of you, Oscar.

There is no point living a life where you're burnt out and have no energy for your family at the end of each day. There is more to life, and that doesn't have to be at the sacrifice of your life. You can make baby steps to changing your life, just like I did with my business. If you want to learn how to use your skills to create a better work life balance for you and your family, then get in touch.

Website: www.kelly-watts-coaching.ck.page/5c5b969d0d

Instagram: www.instagram.com/kellywattscoaching/

LinkedIn: www.linkedin.com/in/kelly-watts-coaching/

Facebook: www.facebook.com/Kellywattscoaching/

CHAPTER 7

By Helen Cooksley

Chartered and Registered Psychologist – Certified Coach – Wellbeing Specialist – Registered Yoga Teacher –Founder and Director of Helen Cooksley Ltd – Menopause Awareness Advocate

If you had known me as a child or young adult, I can quite confidently say you would be surprised to know the adult me was writing a chapter for a book about my mental health journey! To say I was shy, quiet, and private would be an understatement. I always preferred to be out of sight, than centre stage. However, as I sit here reflecting on my journey it is life's challenges and experiences that have shaped the woman I am today. They have led me to this point, as I sit with my fingers lingering over the keyboard with a sense of excitement and trepidation (in a good way!) about what to say. Like Ernest Hemingway said, "In order to write about life first you must live it". Don't get me wrong, there are many parts of my life I would not want to experience again. However, I accept they are part of my story and who knows what my narrative would be, had I run away rather than facing them head on? So, here goes….

Where it all began

On paper I would be considered a fortunate child, raised in a nice rural town with a stay-at-home Mam and a police officer for a father. My gran lived around the corner and there was little crime – in fact, there was very little of anything that occurred. I was an only child and whilst never spoilt, I also never wanted for anything in terms of toys or clothes. However, what would not have been visible was a mother who constantly battled severe bouts of depression, anxiety and obsessive compulsive disorder (OCD), a father who was constantly at work or away, and a child who was anxious, lonely, and helped to care for her mother when she was at her worse. This was the early eighties and people didn't talk about mental health. It was seen as a weakness; something you simply did not tell others- what would they think!!

My Mam experienced PostNatal Depression (PND) and it never resolved, worsening over the years, despite a cocktail of medication, psychiatrists, and treatments. Additionally, she was unable to have any more children, which I believe exacerbated her anxiety and OCD. She was petrified of losing me to the point that it became debilitating for her. On good days she was engaging and fun. On bad days she would cry for hours, beg me not to go to school, and worry constantly that something bad would happen to me, so I was not allowed to go out and play. My grandparents, Aunty, and Cousins were amazing and helped as much as they could. They showed me a glimmer of how everyone else lived and how life could be fun. When I look back there was never any doubt that my Mam loved me. In many ways she loved me too much. Her constant worry did not always allow me to do things children should be doing- playing, getting muddy, making mistakes and learning from them. I had friends but I was never allowed to go far, stay out late, so would often miss out on the full experience. Instead I would usually be helping my Mam check that all of the plug sockets and appliances were turned off and that there were no plastic bags in the house before bed. A set routine that if broken had to be repeated until she felt we were safe.

Because she worried about me so much, I grew up thinking it was better to never worry her further. I would hold on to my feelings or worries like I was protecting state secrets! This became a learned habit and caused me several challenges, especially when hormones started to kick in, and into early adulthood. Some key examples included not telling my parents I suffered terrible nightmares, or that I was bullied in my first year of secondary school- a matter I eventually dealt with myself realising I did have a voice (so not all doom and gloom).

What I did realise at age twelve was that I did not want to be shy or anxious. I didn't want to be the centre of attention, but I definitely did not want it to hold me back. I also knew I didn't want to end up like my Mam, crippled by depression and anxiety. So, after tackling the bully (I will leave it up to you to decide whether this was literal tackling or not- I am not giving away all of my secrets here!), I made a pivotal decision to do something about it. This did not happen overnight, and there were several hurdles to jump, but it acted as my motivation for the several key challenges I had to face in my life.

Everything happens for a reason?

By sixth form, my Mam had managed to control her depression and anxiety better, but she still constantly worried about everything, and especially me. And yes you have guessed it, I also still kept everything to myself fearful of being the cause of additional anxiety or panic attacks for her. I was still working on being bolder and I had made new friends who shared my passion for music. I passed my driving test and got part-time jobs to save money to buy and run a car. I met my first long-term boyfriend who was fun, kind, and encouraged me to open up more. Well, when I say more, it felt a lot to me but it wasn't like I was spilling all my hopes and dreams. There was still work to be done but it was progress!

Whilst sixth form and a car gave me freedom, I craved more, so much more. Every day when I returned home, I felt trapped and anxious, unable to be me – whoever that was – do any of us truly know at 18? I also felt waves of constant guilt for wanting my own life, knowing how challenging it would be for my Mam if I was not around. However, I knew I needed to get out. I remember at points feeling like I would literally explode into a million pieces if I didn't escape. In short, I got my A-Levels and got accepted to study my undergraduate degree in Psychology at a University far enough away to move out of home. I was like a kid in a candy shop! I loved University – the freedom, the parties, the people, and the challenges I faced. I was often still shy, but a lot less than ten year old Helen. I also realised that you don't have to be loud to be heard and that being confident isn't just speaking up- it's 'what' you say that really matters.

At the time I don't think I recognised the significance of studying psychology, however, it became obvious in later life. I was trying to find meaning and answers to my childhood experiences and why my Mam struggled the way she did. At the time I just knew I found the field fascinating. What I didn't know, however, was what I was going to do with it when I graduated. I knew I couldn't afford to do my master's, and I also knew I wanted to maintain my independence. So, I moved to Manchester and got a job. In fact I did several jobs and eventually ended up working in a bank. During that time, I had met a boy, moved in with that boy, and then my Aunty died of terminal cancer. My Aunty was like a second Mam to me, she helped me more than she would ever know when I was growing up. She saw me and encouraged me to find the freedom I craved. Her death hit me hard and the resulting grief threw a curveball I was not prepared for. It pushed me back to my childhood learned habit of holding everything in, with the grief working its way out as apprehension and withdrawal from life. My Mam was also grief stricken as it was her sister who passed away, so I felt I couldn't let her know I was suffering.

Remember my earlier point about my learned habit causing me several challenges into early adulthood? Well, this was definitely one of them! I am in no way saying my grief was worse than anyone else's. However, looking back my inability to talk about it or let it out pushed me to an unhealthy place. I reverted back to childhood Helen. Shortly after my relationship ended with a Manchester boy and I know my lack of openness generally during our relationship was a likely contributor to its downfall.

Somehow though the end of that relationship gave me the kick up the arse I needed. I loved Manchester but made the decision to move back up home. I was annoyed at myself for doing this for some time, as it felt like a failure but I do believe 'everything happens for a reason'. In this case it probably did. While it led to over a decade of constant challenges, it also led to opportunities, self-awareness and growth.

Finding Helen

Fast forward a little further and I was married. Something I never envisaged for myself, given previous relationships. In hindsight I should have listened to my inner voice but hindsight is a wonderful thing, right! I also found myself thinking about my psychology degree. Now was the time to do something with it- I was motivated and ready. I was initially drawn to counselling psychology but then came across a master's course in occupational and organisational psychology. I was drawn to how I could help people and organisations through psychology, applying the evidence base through practical application. I signed up and was able to still work part time. It was tough but worth it and I obtained employment immediately at an organisation that supported law enforcement across the UK. I worked with some wonderful people and led on some great projects – designing and delivering bespoke and large scale recruitment process, managing an-house 360 feedback system, delivering workshops on wellbeing and resilience to those who worked in high pressure and specialist roles, designing a personality assessment process, delivering training, and mentoring aspiring psychologists to name a few. As I developed and grew as a psychologist, it also cemented my passion for helping others grow and develop. I saw its benefits, I noticed that people naturally opened up to me, and that I could facilitate well.

However, while on this amazing journey of learning and self-awareness it soon became a time of sadness, illness, and challenges. It started with my Mam getting cancer after cancer. It became a tragic pattern of diagnosis – treatment - recovery - different cancer diagnosis – treatment – repeat. Every time it was touch and go as to whether she would survive. Each cancer diagnosis felt like I was going through constant grief without any closure, preparing for the inevitable. I faced a string of health challenges myself- measles which almost killed me, and a host of gynaecological issues. You name it, I had it! Fibroids, cysts, heavy periods, and endometriosis that would cause horrendous stabbing pains from nowhere that made me pass out. All of which eventually led to the difficult decision to have an endometrial ablation to manage the endometriosis. It worked but also meant I could not have children.

Sadly, the inevitable did eventually happen for my mam. After nine separate primary cancers, she died at home with family caring for her in her last days. It marked a time of immense sadness, yet also a time of relief. Relief for my Mam as she was ill for so long, and during her last days, as she struggled to catch breath, it was hard beyond belief. But also relief for me - watching someone gradually die and unable to provide any relief is like slow torture. Some of you might think that is a callous feeling, but I did feel a weight lift from me. It was like a lifetime of not wanting to worry my Mam and her pain had dissolved away in that moment. Don't get me wrong, grief hit and so did the guilt over feeling that relief but I eventually worked through that, releasing my emotions were normal.

The date of my Mam's death was also my wedding anniversary and when I reflect back it signified the end of two relationships; the one with my Mam and the one with my now ex-husband. I haven't deliberately omitted my story with him, suffice to say I would need an entire chapter to do that justice! The same applies to the relationship with my Dad! The year my Mam passed, I remember feeling like I was wading through a viscous liquid and seeing the world through fog. I had lost my mojo, my vavavoom, my spark. I put it down to grief and some of it was, but I had this niggling feeling it wasn't just that.

A year later I was still constantly exhausted, couldn't concentrate properly, felt anxious over the most ridiculous things, and ached everywhere. It actually prevented me from applying for a promotion at work. I went to see my doctor and as I ran through my symptoms she sat back and said, "I think you have early menopause!" Scans confirmed both ovaries were inactive. I was 41 years old.

Shortly after my diagnosis my husband announced he had been having an affair. I sought counselling and thrashed through everything!! No stone was left unturned- there were tears, more tears, anger, laughter, and eventually clarity coupled with a sense of calm. It allowed me to focus on just me for the first time. I came out of it with a strong sense of what I wanted and did not want going forward. Counselling and my early menopause diagnosis somehow gave me the freedom to pursue what I wanted most in life. It was like someone had finally turned all of the lights on. I remember a close friend and my cousin saying, "It's nice to have our Helen back again."

In short, I started HRT for the menopause after amazing support from my GP and advice from Dr Louise Newson – HRT was a lifesaver and essential for my future health, but it didn't remove all the symptoms. I still get brain fog and have times where concentration is challenging. I got divorced, got a dog (aka the fur baby), and met a new man (who makes me laugh, and loves me for who I am). I also realised that what I really wanted was to work for myself. I wanted autonomy and to utilise all of my experience and qualifications. Most importantly I wanted to help others navigate their challenges and come out stronger, like I have.

I wanted to help women with hormonal health conditions rethink their challenges, as I had experienced firsthand how it affected my professional identity and career choices. I also wanted to be a yoga teacher as it helped me countless times throughout my life to find harmony and strength. So, I did just that – I started my consultancy business, I trained as a yoga teacher, and I support people personally and in the workplace through coaching and workshops, alongside my consultancy work in leadership, wellbeing, and assessment. I also work with a fantastic colleague on menopause awareness and research and I am planning to complete my professional doctorate. Not quite so shy now!

What I learned along the way

Be kind to yourself – None of us are perfect and that's ok! We all have good and bad days and it can be easy to focus on what is negative over what we can be grateful for. I reflect on what is good in my life during tough times, reframing in a positive light, even if it's small things. I also encourage my clients to do the same, as it helps keep things in perspective. Even when my Mam was in her last days, I was grateful for being there with her. Life does not have to be perfect to still add value.

Despite growing up as someone who never shared her feelings, I know from a personal and professional perspective, that talking really does help! As I reflect on childhood me who would bottle everything up, it was not healthy or helpful. Now I share my feelings, my concerns, and my dreams. When I deliver workshops on how to build healthy coping strategies, or coaching clients, I always integrate the importance of talking and a good support network. Conversation can be the catalyst for real self-discovery if you are talking with the right person, which leads me on to my next point…

Avoid toxic relationships and people, where possible. One of my rules now is to avoid those who drag me down, drain me, or compete with me. Instead I aim to surround myself with those I trust, lift me up, make me laugh, have my back, and empower me to grow. I also encourage my clients to do the same. Don't allow a person to negatively impact your life, where it's avoidable. It's essential for your wellbeing – "you only live once, but if you do it right, once is enough" (Mae West).

Taking time for yourself is not selfish, it can be essential, and something I need more than ever since early menopause. As I reflect on my life I was literally living off cortisol and adrenaline for over a decade! As a psychologist, I know all too well that it is not a healthy or sustainable cocktail over time! Our bodies and minds are so interconnected, if we ignore one then the other will eventually send us a warning. One will eventually say no. I strive to set healthy boundaries and encourage my clients to find ways to do the same. When I do yoga, breathwork, or walk my dog it allows time for reflection and an opportunity to reset. When I step away from the busy, is when I have my best ideas!

It's the challenges we face that help us to grow and develop. I see this with my clients during my coaching sessions and workshops. Personally, I know it's the challenges I faced that have led me to become the psychologist and woman I am today. I also recognise that I use my own professional skills as a psychologist, coach, and yoga teacher to not only help others, but to manage my life more effectively and remain resilient throughout the tough times. I know my triggers and I know what works for me and what doesn't by trying different strategies, accepting the uncomfortable experiences, and reframing them into growth and self-awareness.

Finally, whilst my early menopause or journey may not resonate with your experiences, I believe that no matter what the physical or mental health challenge, life is short, don't look back and wonder, 'what if I had only….' Your greatest challenges could also become some of your greatest strengths. So, I'm going to leave you with a question to reflect on, if you will please indulge me.

Ask yourself, what would happen if you did nothing about your personal, professional, or health challenges for a month, six months, a year? Can you afford to leave them unexplored?

If you would like to know more about my journey or ways to better manage your own wellbeing or menopause journey, I would love to hear from you.

You can find me here:

Website:

LinkedIn:

Instagram:

Eventbrite (for workshops and events):

CHAPTER 8

By Amy Mostert

Courage, above all things, is the first quality of a warrior." — Carl von Clausewitz.

I can't believe I'm lucky enough to realise my dream and write this book chapter with all these amazing, courageous authors. Hi, I'm Amy—a mum to two gorgeous children who light up my soul, a dog-mum, wife, and former primary school teacher turned serial entrepreneur.

I'm proudly neurodiverse and have three diagnosed chronic illnesses: M.E/CFS, fibromyalgia, and Costochondritis (I bet you had to look that last one up!). Throughout this chapter, I will take you on the journey that led me to where I am now, through all the trials, hardships, joys, and lessons—everything that made me the warrior I am today. I've dreamt of writing a book for many years. I've started, stopped, and procrastinated — a dream I just never quite found the courage to pursue. Speaking these words and sharing some of the hardest moments of my life has brought me to tears many times during this process. I've had to take it slowly, resting as I crashed each time a new memory or trauma surfaced and healed. Thinking about how much I've overcome and how I continue to battle on as that warrior every day inspired me to keep writing. This journey is not easy; it's not for the faint-hearted. But every day, I wake up and draw on the strength I know I have to live the best day I can, however, that might look.

Over the years, I've been developing and adding to my passion project business, "Mum Wife Warrior," to make it everything I had needed and had looked for over the years so that it might help others just like me. I'm going to take you through my journey now, and hopefully, at the end, you'll want to continue following me and the rest of my as-yet-unwritten path.

Diagnosis and Early Challenges

As I write this chapter, I'm 45 years old. I was first diagnosed with M.E/CFS when I was just 15, and the journey to that diagnosis is a little hazy in my mind; however, the emotions and feelings are still very much alive. I don't remember everything that led up to the moment when I sat in the chair and the consultant told me that I had M.E/CFS. I do remember being constantly ill from a young age. Anytime I got too excited or did too much, it would always result in being unwell and missing out on many exciting parts of being a child. I was diagnosed with Fibromyalgia ten years ago whilst pregnant with my second child. Don't get me wrong—I had an amazing childhood with a lot of fun and many friends. But even from an early age, there were compromises in what I was capable of doing. I was fortunate that my parents advocated for me; they fought for a diagnosis to help me. I clearly remember sitting down and being told I had M.E., then being told there really wasn't much that they could do: rest when needed; exercise; eat a good diet. Unfortunately, in my experiences since then, there hasn't been much progress in what they can do to help. At that time, it was a mixture of relief that it had a name and complete despair of having an illness with no cure at the age of 15. The next few years featured many lessons and challenges. I've had moments where I felt normal and lived like any other teenager, but there were also moments of the lowest of lows and the darkest times.

***"Courage isn't only fighting your circumstances; sometimes making peace with your circumstances requires more courage."* — Sonali Dev**

After the diagnosis of M.E/CFS, the next five years shaped me for the following 25. I had to learn to adjust to my life, pace myself, and overcome many bad moments. The worst time for me, which has had a lasting impact, was probably when I was around 17/18 years old. If you knew me then, it is likely that this moment in time skipped by, and you had no idea what was happening. I took any opportunity where I felt normal to put a smile on my face and live for that moment as best I could. But in reality, I was struggling. The M.E became severe; I lost weight, going down to 5 1/2 stone. I struggled to walk to the bathroom and slept so much, spending a lot of time in bed. My mental health deteriorated to a point where I wasn't sure I could go on; I just wanted it all to end, to disappear into the sky and be free and at peace.

As I rested and nourished myself, I began to do more, move more, and see a light. Each day, I thought positively, focusing on one thing I could do tomorrow to move towards living again. This took great strength and commitment. This was the moment the warrior in me was born. This inner warrior is whom I now look to and remind myself of even now: how strong, determined, and amazing she was. I remind myself that anytime I need her, she is there, and she has my back. I didn't do anything too radical. I just looked after myself—rested, slept, and nourished my mind and body. I researched the best food to eat and what to avoid. I cut out all the bad things I could, practised meditation, reconnected with my inner child, and nourished her soul. I did everything to love myself and give myself the tools and grace to heal. This is what saved me. As I type this, I am so proud of myself. I knew I needed to do all of this again, and how I have once again saved myself all these years later.

***"The flower that blooms in adversity is the most rare and beautiful of all."* FaZhou, Mulan**

Friendships and Relationships

In all honesty, I am always learning and evolving when it comes to relationships. As I come to understand myself better and why I respond the way I do, I realise that I sometimes become a martyr, thinking I can do it all alone. But it runs deeper than this. To have a chronic illness and fully lean on someone is difficult. I've been contacted many times by friends recently diagnosed, looking for advice on dealing with the illness and explaining it to their partners. The truth is, they won't walk in our shoes and will never fully understand. For this, we need to give them grace, communicate, and not hide. Easier said than done, and this takes practice from both sides.

I very easily fall into the trap of masking and pretending that I am okay, just getting through the day. Instead, I should say I am not okay. Today, I need help with x, y, and z so I can be well tomorrow. I am learning and growing each day just like you. Asking for help felt like admitting defeat like the illness had won. Now I realise the opposite is true. With rest and support, I can recover faster, do more, and build stronger relationships instead of hiding the uselessness, darkness, and despair I often felt inside.

I used to hide in bathrooms, cupboards, and in the car, silently screaming or crying, rocking back and forth, thinking I couldn't live like this anymore - let it win, to just take me now and end this pain and misery. These days are much fewer and farther between now. This is hard to write and admit out loud! These days do still happen, but I have found strength in honesty to free myself each time I speak about it and what I need. Now, I rest when I need to.

I've created a business and job where I can rest and sleep comfortably around my needs. I've opened up to friends about being unwell and why I can't do things sometimes. To my surprise, they get it and appreciate the honesty, rather than feeling like they are being brushed off.

It makes all of my relationships stronger when I admit I need help, vocalise that I don't feel well, or that I am tired. That I need assistance with tasks, work, cleaning, or just silence. It makes me a better person to be around when I rest and look after my needs. I once viewed this as selfish and indulgent, but now my eyes are open. I realise this self-care allows me to be the best version of myself for me and for those around me who deserve the best version of me, too.

***"Sometimes asking for help is the most meaningful example of self-reliance."* — From the poem "Sometimes" by Cory Booker**

Parenting

One of my biggest drivers for this journey to wellness and managing this illness is my family. They keep me going in the bleakest of moments. Having children has been a huge journey and a driving force behind me putting one foot in front of the other. I refuse to succumb to this fate, this life of chronic illness. There has to be a better way—a way to get to the life you want and the solutions that allow you to live fully. This is the passion behind my business and journey: helping people get to where I am faster and easier than I did. I loved becoming a mum and cherished each moment, but my goodness, it came with guilt, and it really shouldn't. We apologise and feel guilty about so many parts of our lives so often that it becomes a reflex. I stopped apologising long ago. I won't apologise for being me anymore or for walking through this life.

Mum guilt can be all-consuming! In full transparency, overcoming this mum guilt is a work in progress, and each day it becomes less, I see myself and my children a little happier. Now, we replace guilt with boundaries and fulfilment of our actual needs—not what I think I should be doing. We talk more, and I have learned that taking time out and modelling self-love, along with keeping friend dates, looking after myself, being still sometimes, and asserting boundaries results in all our needs being met instead of me trying to fix things and be everything all the time. This feels so freeing, and it's how we live now (well, mostly—we do still have some moments of failure or learning).

There are many people already living like this, and I am in awe of them, using them as my inspiration. The world has changed and is changing again. I am so happy to see this and love the possibilities it brings; we really can have it all, and I love this!

Starting and Running a Business

Starting my entrepreneurial journey has been everything I needed it to be, but it doesn't mean it hasn't challenged or tested me along the way. The main reason for moving from employment to self-employment was driven by my need to be home for my children and the cost, both financially and physically. Going to work no longer made sense, so I stopped. It was a risk, but I knew I would make it work for us. I have always been a little stubborn when my mind is set. Self-employment has looked different at each stage. I started my own messy play business with another mum. It gave us exactly what we needed and came to a natural end when the children started school. We sold the company and passed the baton to another mum. It was a brilliant experience, and I learned so much about business. The physicality was a little much some days, but

I factored this in and rested as much as possible between classes. I moved on to various roles working for other people. While I learned a lot and gained skills, there were definite traumas and life lessons that came along with the good moments. Along the way, I have grown and developed my mindset, values, knowledge, and inner circle of incredible people. I highly recommend self-employment. I can tailor my day to my needs, be in the comfort of my own home with blankets, hot water bottles, and comfortable clothes, and work at my desk, on the couch, or in bed—whatever my body needs. If I need to nap I can, I have my kitchen freely available to get the nutrition I need at any moment if I feel I am flagging and need a boost. I dictate the hours and the time I need.

Don't get me wrong; you are still answerable to clients and deadlines, but how you work and set up your working week is all your decision. Just set the expectations from the start. This life is not for everyone, and while the above sounds like a dream, you do have to be disciplined, motivated, and mentally strong. It can be worrying not having a consistent paycheck each month and the instability at first. The onus is on you to find and keep clients. You can feel lonely and isolated some days, so building a community and network of other entrepreneurs around you is crucial. Everything in life has the good and the bad; you have to weigh up what works for you and if you can take the compromises it brings with it.

I have been working like this for the best part of ten years, and I don't think I could go back to a traditional role anymore. This lifestyle gives me everything I need and want from a career. It allows me to be fully me, to live how I need to, not how I am expected to. I can take time off when

I need to and have the freedom to look after myself in the best way possible. I don't think I can describe how blessed I feel to be in this position. It didn't happen overnight, but it is a leap and decision I will forever be proud of. I took a chance on myself, knew what I needed, and went for it. The warrior in me shone through once again.

"Sometimes the smallest step in the right direction ends up being the biggest step of your life. Tiptoe if you must, but take a step." —
Naeem Callaway

Mindset, Balance, and Holistic Wellness

I have gotten it wrong so many times, but I hope that I learn from each moment in my journey. Each time I wake up, I try to learn something new, whether it is a tip, trick, piece of knowledge, or realisation about me and my journey. I like to evolve and grow each day to be the best version of myself when I go to sleep. I am on a new path to finding and trying all the natural and holistic healing methods I can. I have tried many—from sound baths to tuning forks, to Reiki—and the effects have been profound and positive. This is an area I will continue to explore alongside medication when needed and it will be an important part of my journey to come.

This is just a glimpse into my journey. While writing, I realised I have so much to say and share so I hope you will find me and follow along. I feel like I have barely brushed the surface, but I hope it gives someone the hope, understanding, and peace they were missing and needed before they started reading.

To end my chapter, I would like to leave you with some of the best advice I have been given over the years:

Have a growth mindset: Embrace the challenges and changes that will come up. Seek solutions that empower and move you forward.

Take a moment to do something each day to fill your cup: Rest, read, move, have fun, and do something just for you.

Eat well: We are what we eat, so fuel yourself well for optimum performance. Don't forget to hydrate each day as well.

Move, anyway you can: Stretch, walk, do gentle exercise. However small, just keep moving. (Disclaimer: if you have severe M.E or pain, I appreciate this is impossible at times—I've been there. But when you can, keep moving.)

Positive Mental Attitude (PMA): This is something my mother has always said to me. Each time I need a reset or boost, I say this to myself. Even in the dark, there is a light. Even in the storm, there is a rainbow. In the hard times, there are good times. Keep positive; this is the one thing that has always seen me through and brought me strength when I needed it.

Ask for help, seek support, and find your community: we don't have to walk through this alone. Find strength in each other and lift each other up. Look to others when you can no longer hold yourself up. We are warriors together, and we have you in our hearts and thoughts.

Be selfish: Sometimes it is okay to be selfish! Except it isn't being selfish—it is loving yourself above all else, and this is empowerment. You are enough and perfect just the way you are.

Travel well: Not everyone can take this journey—you are the warriors who can shine a light for those who follow behind.

"Life isn't about waiting for the storm to pass; it's about learning to dance in the rain." **— Vivian Greene**

Where to find me:

Facebook - www.facebook.com/mumwifewarrior

Instagram - www.instagram.com/mumwifewarrior/

Website – www.mumwifewarrior.com/

QR Code:

COURAGE

"COURAGE DOESN'T ALWAYS ROAR. SOMETIMES COURAGE IS THE QUIET VOICE AT THE END OF THE DAY SAYING, I WILL TRY AGAIN TOMORROW."

- MARY ANNE RADMACHER

CHAPTER 9

By Sarah Carruthers

Befriending your shadow, awakening your light

Sometimes life throws you unexpected curve balls. And sometimes how you react takes you by surprise.

Have you ever encountered resistance when trying to make positive changes in your life? Acted "out of character" in frustration, anger, desire? Done something embarrassing? Ever feared "am I a bad person?" Or found yourself triggered by someone else's behaviour? These moments can offer a glimpse into the parts of ourselves we try to ignore or suppress—our shadow.

Your shadow is the part of you that lies beneath the carefully curated image you show to the world—the raw, naked, unadorned, vulnerable self, often burdened with shame, guilt, and a sense of exposure. Just like the story of Adam and Eve who after eating the forbidden fruit, felt shame and tried to cover their nakedness, we too hide aspects of ourselves out of fear of judgement and rejection. This shadow side often comes out at the most difficult times of our life.

Allow me to introduce your shadow self

The shadow represents everything that bothers, unsettles, disturbs, or repels us about others and ourselves—the traits and aspects we find unpleasant or struggle to acknowledge. Carl Jung said, *"our shadow is the person we would rather not be,"* so it can feel uncomfortable when you meet it for the first time. We are conditioned to fear our dark side and when we catch ourselves going there, we run, repress, or ignore it like an ostrich sticking its head in the sand—hoping it will disappear when we look out again.

However, even if we ignore our shadow, it doesn't disappear—it lurks beneath the surface, ready to surprise you at the worst possible moments. Like holding a beach ball underwater, that eventually pops up and smacks you in the face, the more we push it down, the more mischievously it finds a way to sneak out; like blurting out a secret, snapping at a loved one, or sabotaging our own efforts with procrastination or self-doubt. We tell ourselves that if we ever fully revealed our quirky, flawed selves, even those closest to us would turn away, so we do everything we can to bury it deep inside.

What if your shadow was actually your friend and ally?

Jung viewed the shadow as a gateway to the collective unconscious, a treasure trove of creativity, brilliance, insight, and wisdom. He claimed that by hiding parts of ourselves, we limit access to our "golden shadow"—the full range of emotions, ideas, abilities and creative potential. The reality is that by integrating these hidden aspects we free up energy, boost self-awareness, enrich relationships, enhance happiness and our ability to live out our dreams.

Jung described the shadow as a "sparring partner"—a mentor and guide that reveals the true magnificence within us. Far from being an enemy, it provides a rich opportunity for growth, helping us develop into who we are meant to be.

So how does our shadow develop?

We are born innocent, trusting and unashamed, fully dependent on our caregivers. As we grow, our temperament, attachment styles, and experiences shape our personalities as a way to keep ourselves seen, soothed, safe and secure, often at the expense of our true selves.

As children, we quickly learn which behaviours are acceptable and which are not e.g. in a strict, rule-bound environment, being "good" might bring love and safety, while stepping out of line can lead to rejection and shame, so then traits that are wild, spontaneous, or impulsive can get pushed into the shadow.

Cultural and societal expectations also shape our shadows. Boys are often taught to hide emotions and be tough, suppressing sensitivity and vulnerability. Women may be encouraged to be modest and selfless, leading to the repression of sexual desire, assertiveness, and anger.

While these strategies help us to survive, they can also confine us to a limited version of who we truly are. The harsh reality is that repressing and avoiding our shadow only amplifies its power, leading to greater pain, suffering, and a deep sense of regret.

Fortunately, we are not bound to these self-imposed limits. As Viktor Frankl wrote, *"Between stimulus and response, there is a space. In that space lies our freedom and our power to choose our response."* Befriending our shadow allows us to move beyond reactive patterns, reclaim our power, and evolve into a more authentic and wiser self.

What is shadow work?

Shadow work is the name given to reconnecting with the parts of ourselves we've rejected or suppressed, embracing both our light and dark sides with acceptance and love, and transforming a divided self into a unified whole. As Jung wrote, true wholeness comes from integrating our shadow, leading to greater personal growth and a more fulfilling life.

Your shadow holds significant inner power and freedom which is only accessible when you explore its hidden depths. It takes courage to do that, to go against our instinct to hide away for protection.

The reality is that by healing our shadow, we feel valued and loved, shifting how we see ourselves and how we interact with the world.

Would you like to meet your Shadow?

Find a quiet safe space, where you can reflect inwardly.

Exercise:

Close your eyes and transport yourself back to your childhood. Reflect on a behaviour/trait that was strongly disapproved of and shut down.

For instance, if your family valued academic success, you might have felt pressure to excel or rebel against expectations. If your family prized conformity and avoided risk-taking, you might have developed a hidden craving for adventure/creativity.

Reflect on what was discouraged/longed for.

Visualise the part of yourself that was pushed aside/hidden because it didn't align with expectations. This is most likely part of your shadow.

My story

Over the years I had been confronted by my Shadow on many occasions. Sometimes, a fleeting encounter, barely noticeable, disguised as a moment of temper, disappointment, discarded as a momentary lapse, enabling it to withdraw back into the darkness. But in February 2019 my Shadow came out into the light and I came face to face with part of myself I really didn't like.

My husband Rob, an avid mountain biker, collided with a tree at 40 km/h. Unfortunately, the tree emerged victorious, resulting in a serious concussion that eventually evolved into post-concussion syndrome. Our lives were transformed overnight. His injury forced me into a challenging new reality, stripping away the spontaneity and freedom I cherished. With two young children to care for, I felt trapped and overwhelmed, instead of loved and empathised with. The reality of constant caregiving, a low-stimulus environment, and financial pressures triggered my deepest fears and anxieties. Rob needed my unwavering support which caused me to come face to face with my shadow—and it wasn't pleasant.

I convinced myself that not only were my desires and my freedom being sacrificed, but that I was losing my identity under the crushing weight of responsibility. The loneliness was deep and profound, and I was tormented by guilt and shame for how I felt. This was not the mindset of a loving wife. My instinct was to turn away from my shadow's smoke signals—to bargain with it, push it aside, deny this was happening and keep going. I just wanted to go back to the way things were.

Instead, I chose to work with a coach to acknowledge and befriend the parts of me I had kept under wraps. In this work, I encountered a separate being within me—a six-year-old blonde girl who felt alone and unloved. This young self carried the deep-seated pain and isolation I had suppressed for years. She was barely holding it together. No wonder she came out so powerfully— she couldn't stay quiet any longer. Through coaching, journaling, and my faith, I started to understand this vulnerable part of myself. I nurtured her with love and compassion, healing aspects that were marred by fear, resistance, and shame. I learned to embrace her, offer her acceptance, and integrate her into my life.

Exploring my shadow at this time had been a hugely challenging journey, but led to a profound integration, creativity, lightness, and a deep sense of peace. But just as I was making progress, we received the devastating news that Rob had stage IV lung cancer. I was going to need all the strength I could muster.

Supporting Rob through his brutal three-year walk with cancer, which ended with his death in November 2023 reinforced a crucial realisation: befriending my shadow was not merely a survival tactic, but essential for my own growth and healing, and that of my children and ultimately, vital for my clients' journeys too.

***"One does not become enlightened by the light but by making the darkness light."* Carl Jung**

I shudder to think how life might have unfolded if I had tried to shut my shadow away during that crucial time. It was as if she knew she needed to be heard.

If you are not your story, who are you?

Stepping outside the familiar story you've been telling yourself can be unsettling, stirring fears of losing your identity, sense of belonging, or self-worth. Shame thrives in secrecy, and Brené Brown teaches that the antidote is connection and openness.

By owning our story and sharing it with someone we trust, we reduce shame's power and promote healing. Embracing vulnerability allows us to live fully.

By integrating both your light and darkness, you create a positive ripple effect that enhances not just your life, but also the world around you.

***"Owning our story can be hard but not nearly as difficult as spending our lives running from it. Embracing our vulnerabilities and our imperfections is a way to be truly free."* Brené Brown**

Shadow work offers profound benefits such as overcoming barriers, finding emotional healing, boosting creativity, improving relationships, and achieving a sense of radical wholeness. Failing to address your shadow can impact various life areas and can lead to wasting vital energy on bad habits and self-sabotaging behaviours—aka the Jekyll and Hyde dynamic. For example, Will Smith's public outburst at the Oscars demonstrated how repressed emotions, when ignored for too long, can emerge in destructive ways.

My own experience showed that developing a consistent and mindful relationship with your shadow is crucial. So the next time your shadow shows up and makes itself known, be courageous and meet it head on.

When we bravely face our fears, with expert support and the right tools, we discover that it leads not to shame or limitation but that it opens the door to compassion, and freedom. Our shadow longs to be acknowledged, and as it heals and feels accepted, it brings valuable wisdom and uncovers qualities that were previously hidden. This process initiates a profound and transformative journey toward integration, balance and wholeness.

It will not necessarily change the circumstances you find yourself in—but will radically change your interaction with it. It gave me a way through and enabled me to keep on that journey.

Are you ready to embark on this transformative journey?

If you have experienced deep trauma, addiction, or mental health issues (including anxiety or depression) it's essential to address these with a trained therapist/coach before starting shadow work.

For added support and/or guidance, The Luminosity Project **(www.theluminosityproject.nz/)** offers trauma-informed coaches skilled in polyvagal therapy to guide you safely and appropriately. Please reach out if we can support you in any way.

Your shadow may communicate through symbolism, images, or metaphors, but it can also emerge in your ideas, intuition, and dreams. As you move forward, approach this with openness and flexibility, noting recurring themes that highlight specific wounds. Focus on what resonates most emotionally.

Exercise:

Note: If any part of this exercise becomes overwhelming/ intense, just pause and return when ready.

Let's begin by tuning into our shadow:

1. *Find a safe and quiet place where you can reflect.*
2. *Close your eyes. Identify something you would never want anyone else to know about you—something you're ashamed of/ feel guilty about/ have hidden from others.*

3. *What does this secret/longing/fantasy/mistake/vulnerability look, feel, and sound like? Safely observe it and be aware, non-judgementally. What do you notice?*
4. *As you gently dip your toe into this experience, give this hidden part of yourself a distinct face and form—one that embodies the aspects you're reluctant to show.*
5. *As you compassionately observe this personification, notice your feelings and what this part needs/longs for (probably something it has never been given).*
6. *Listen to its needs. Let it communicate. Offer it safety, love, kindness and understanding.*
7. *Acknowledge your role in its pain and apologise for not providing the care and protection it needed.*
8. *Ask if there's anything you can do to build trust and show that you're committed to understanding and integrating this part of yourself.*
9. *Open your eyes and jot down any important insights.*

Your shadow's deepest desire is acknowledgment; to be seen and heard. Regularly engaging with and validating this part of yourself helps connect with its wisdom. This isn't about letting your shadow control you, but about giving it a voice—a seat at the table—integrating it into your inner dialogue.

Think of it as nurturing a close friendship—spending 10-15 minutes daily connecting with it, transforming it into a supportive ally. This lifelong discipline enhances self-awareness and fosters personal growth.

Seven key considerations to help you build a relationship with your shadow

1. Start by cultivating self-regulation, self compassion, and curiosity

Engaging with your hidden parts can trigger intense emotions and responses. Without effective self-regulation, you might react defensively or slip into fight, flight, or freeze modes. Begin by bringing your nervous system into a calm alert state by grounding yourself or use a practice like coherent breathing (breathe in fully, slowly and evenly, finding a rhythm that suits you, such as a 5-second inhale followed by a 5-second exhale). You can find these at **www.theluminosityproject.nz**

Self-compassion and curiosity allow you to approach your shadow with kindness and openness. Set a nurturing tone for your inner dialogue with affirmations like, *"I approach this work with warmth, patience, and understanding, just as I would for a dear friend facing a tough time."* When encountering challenging or uncomfortable aspects of yourself, embrace a curious, beginner's mind with a tone of inclusion e.g. *"I'm curious, what is this part of me trying to communicate? What can I learn?"*

2. Practice self-awareness

Self-awareness means observing and understanding your behaviours, thoughts, and feelings clearly and openly. When triggered, pause and notice your emotional responses and thoughts without judgment. Practice viewing yourself as an impartial witness, asking questions like,

"What triggered this reaction? How are my thoughts affecting my feelings and actions?"

3. Pay attention to your reactions and projections

Observing your reactions to others can reveal different aspects of your shadow. Strong negative feelings or intense admiration often reflect parts of yourself you might be avoiding. For example, disliking a friend's controlling behaviour might mirror your own fears of losing control.

Reflect on what triggers strong reactions for you and ask, *"What is my earliest experience with this quality? What beliefs do I hold about it? What story am I telling myself?"* (For more introspection, explore our shadow work prompts at https://www.theluminosityproject.nz/)

4. Embrace honesty and have courage to admit the truth

Honesty, integrity and courage are essential for confronting parts of yourself you might prefer to ignore or hide from. Embrace the discomfort, as you openly recognise and acknowledge your flaws, fears, and desires.

Practice *"feel it to heal it"* by tuning into physical sensations—like tension or numbness—during strong emotions. Ask, *"If this emotion could speak, what would it say? What is this sensation trying to reveal?"* Stay present with these sensations without rushing to analyse or fix them, knowing they will pass naturally within 90 seconds if you avoid the temptation to hook into the story and meaning surrounding it.

5. **Dialogue with your inner self**

Conversing with different aspects of yourself may feel unusual at first, but it's essential work in transforming your shadow from a source of conflict into a valuable resource, enhancing self-awareness and fostering growth. Techniques such as journaling, embodied intelligence coaching, inner child work, and Interactive Drawing Therapy can help you bring these parts into awareness and facilitate meaningful inner dialogue. The Luminosity Project https://www.theluminosityproject.nz/ can help you with this.

6. **Log your discoveries**

Maintain a journal—written, video, or audio—to record your observations, insights, and emotions. This practice helps track progress, identify patterns, and deepen your understanding of your inner experiences. Regularly review your entries to gain clarity, reinforce growth, and guide future exploration.

7. **Practice gratitude at every level**

To enhance your well-being and self-improvement, integrate gratitude into your self-exploration. Reflect on what you appreciate and understand intellectually (head); the emotional growth, values and connections you are thankful for (heart); and gratitude for the intuitive insights, needs and motivations that have arisen (gut).

For a practical, neuroscience-based approach, explore The Ultimate Gratitude Journal: A practical neuroscience approach to rewiring your brain to be healthier and happier at:

www.theluminosityproject.nz/the-ultimate-gratitude-journal

This resource teaches effective gratitude practices, supported by research, to foster calm alertness and deeper well-being, while improving your connections with yourself and others.

Shadow work is essential for personal growth

The shadow realm is fluid, symbolic, and often elusive, encompassing the hidden and suppressed parts of ourselves that shape our behaviour and emotions. The shadow is not a fearsome adversary but an essential part of each of us. Its power is significant, yet the power of radical wholeness is infinitely bigger. By acknowledging, befriending and loving our shadow, we move beyond the surface, integrating all facets of ourselves, and tapping into deeper dimensions of our intelligence. As Leonard Cohen writes *"the cracks are where the light gets in"*, so we embrace the beauty of our imperfections and our vulnerability, sharing authentically with those we trust.

Nurturing our shadow and valuing our true self, enables us to show up in radical wholeness, with no need for masks or pretence. It unlocks limitless potential for growth and leads to a more authentic and fulfilling life.

Our holistic approach at The Luminosity Project offers clarity and compassion in your shadow work, helping to reveal your radiant potential. If you're interested in how we can support you, via coaching, spiritual direction, workshops or coach trainings please feel free to reach out at The Luminosity Project or **info@theluminosityproject.nz**

And so we encourage you to embrace this journey with us, knowing that extraordinary potential awaits just beneath the surface, even in the most challenging of times.

"You are meant to shine and manifest the glory within you. By embracing your own light, you inspire others to do the same. As you liberate yourself from fear, your presence will help liberate others as well." **Marianne Williamson**

CHAPTER 10

By Andreas Dating Coach

The World of Love is a Circus

Imagine you're at a circus.

Imagine the lights, the smells, the fun, the laughter, the thrills, and the suspense...

Now, close your eyes and imagine for a moment about which act or performer you would be and why? Feel free to write down your answer to my question in as much detail as possible while it's fresh in your mind. Its significance will be clarified later.

A Serial Lover

I'm an incurable romantic; a lover, not a fighter; a serial lover, in fact. I've never hesitated to use the L-word when appropriate, and while I've had my fair share of love, it has often turned sour. Each time, one might think I'd be pushed further away from commitment. Yet, that is not the case. I would take a break, dust myself off, have some fun, and then dive back in with someone new. I've often wondered why people fall in and out of love with the same person so easily, often ending with so much angst and resentment.

I say this with relief: I was never hung up on my exes. Each break was clean, albeit painful, filled with heartache and a degree of shame. I despise failure and felt like one each time. I pity those yearning to win back their exes, trapped in limbo. When approaching new relationships, I maintained an optimistic mindset, offering my new partner commitment, loyalty, and positivity; at least, that was my intention. After all, love was meant to be forever, right? Well, forever until it fizzled out again, and we grew apart, wanting different things and disagreeing on values and careers. The list became endless! There was no cheating, but enough issues between us to lead to a breakup. In my eyes, I was just another shameful statistic: engaged twice, married and divorced once.

By my late 40s, I found myself single, without a partner or children. My ancestral family tree seemed a dead end, with my lonesome name at the end of it, a painful thought. My Greek Cypriot roots felt strained, despite being born and raised in London. My parents would have loved for me to settle down with a nice Greek girl (through introduction) and give them grandchildren. I had my own mind and found it embarrassing to be spoon-fed a life partner. Growing up in the UK, the thought felt philistine to me. I was more than capable of finding my own partners, and they certainly weren't always Greek, although my first two were, as I tried to appease the cultural norm of our tight-knit community. Continuing the family tradition of naming my first-born after my father was a must. I loved the idea of naming my son George, as my father was named after his grandfather, and I was named after mine, Andreas, and so on. I took pride in this tradition and would share it with every prospective partner, usually on the first date.

One Common Denominator: Me!

The truth was my exes were genuinely beautiful, wonderful women, everything any man could wish for. It would have been easier to accept if they weren't nice people, but that wasn't the case. So, what was the problem? Clearly, there was one common denominator in all my relationships: me! While I believe I possess many good qualities, I also have numerous faults, or perhaps I was simply hard work.

As a Virgo man, my personality is shaped by a mix of traits that define who I am, some beneficial and some challenging in relationships. My perfectionism drives me to strive for excellence, but it can also lead to high expectations for myself and others. I often find myself overly critical, especially of myself, and I freeze when anxiety about making a mistake or not being perfect consumes me. Procrastination follows, turning into a debilitating cycle. This perfectionist streak sometimes makes it hard to appreciate the small imperfections that make us human.

I want things my way, or the highway, and I've uttered that phrase more times than I'd like to admit, only to despise myself for it. It's an unattractive trait, as I often prefer to do everything myself rather than trust others, leaving my partners feeling inadequate. I can also be self-righteous and opinionated, which sometimes manifests as being overly critical. Instead of offering constructive feedback, I might focus too much on what's wrong, which can hurt those I care about. My attention to detail, while helpful, can lead me to nitpick things that don't matter in the grand scheme of things, frustrating my partners.

Reliability is generally a positive trait, yet it creates pressure for me to always be the rock in the relationship, which isn't easy. I have learned to let go and trust my partner's abilities more. One area where I've improved significantly is active listening. To say I used to be very bad at it is an understatement, but there's still room for improvement.

On Reflection

When my longest relationship of 13 years ended and I moved out, I was determined to work on myself in every way possible. I needed to understand who I was and what I wanted in life. I questioned what I had achieved. There I was, broke and depressed, having not long lost my multi-million-pound nightclub and promotions business, which had taken its toll on me. I was reliant on family support to keep me sane and was grateful for it. I could sympathise with people who would contemplate a way out as a solution but thankfully I had the strength and the support I needed around me.

I moved in with my much younger cousin, who was also single, and he motivated me to get fit again by going to the gym. It was a great distraction, socialising with his friends and family, all 20-odd years younger than me. Luckily, I managed to fit in. While most people my age were contemplating retirement, I was focused on what to do next. I was stuck. I had to knuckle down, helping my father manage his construction business while using my spare time to work on myself, my wants and, more importantly, my needs.

Friends and family were accustomed to my changing jobs and partners, which became entertaining for them, akin to an explorer sharing their exploits. I've done many things, starting young. I used to entertain my parents' customers in their hairdressing salon at age three, strumming my guitar and singing Beatles songs. This even landed me on the front page of the local newspaper when a journalist customer got the scoop. As a young entrepreneur about nine years old, I would sell raffle tickets in the shop for prizes like haircuts and highlights, with my parents none the wiser until the draw occurred. By the age of 15, I was obsessed with DJing, having built my mobile setup and started collecting soul and disco vinyl records. It led to DJing in nightclubs at 17 and becoming a resident club DJ every summer in Cyprus into my mid-20s. I loved entertaining people, controlling a crowd; it was exhilarating! Back then, it wasn't a career per se, but during university, it provided extra cash for more records. I studied Architecture, while wanting to become an interior designer specialising in nightclubs. I designed my first club at 22, my second at 27, and then my own two clubs in my late 30s. When my architectural business shut down during the UK recession in the early

90s, I ventured into club promotions with my cousin Pete and brother Kristos, growing a club empire out of retro disco, Starsky & Hutch 70sfunksouljazzdisco. We won best club promotion in the UK two years running and expanded overseas with franchises in Buenos Aires, Argentina, and Ayia Napa, Cyprus to name a few. It was fun and surreal at times, becoming friends with my childhood idol, Antonio Fargas (aka Huggy Bear), and entertaining over 10,000 customers a week with plenty of travel and partying. We produced a compilation music CD, and our own theme tune with Huggy when I signed with Virgin Records. But it all came to an abrupt and painful end. The bubble burst, money disappeared; the only ones who profited were the lawyers, who in hindsight, provided poor advice. Lesson learned.

As I mentioned, I've pursued a colourful variety of jobs. I've been an Architectural designer, a club DJ, a radio presenter, a club and radio station owner, a music producer, a builder/project manager, a photographer, a delivery driver, a waiter, a sales assistant, and a dating and relationship mentor. The last role gives me the most satisfaction, even more than DJing. Don't get me wrong, whipping a crowd into a frenzy is thrilling, but the joy I derive from helping people find love and their ideal partners surpasses it.

Growth

Through adversity and failure, I discovered growth. I was able to start anew. I agree with Tony Robbins when he says, "Life doesn't happen to you; it happens for you." All my vast experiences had got me where I was now. I spent hours contemplating how I would leave my mark on the world. I knew I would; I just didn't yet know how, yet. I also yearned for companionship. I love feminine essence, I love women, and being single again deepened my desire for female company and attention. Don't get me wrong; my male friends and family are fantastic, but I craved a connection with women, prioritising dates. This is why my relationships with women often flourished quickly; I gave them so much attention, putting them first, which made it easy to build connections. But this time, things would be different.

I needed to break my cycle. The dating culture had changed, and there was unlimited choice of women on internet dating sites. There, I didn't have to reveal I was "damaged goods" from my past engagements and marriages. Instead, I could present myself as the best version of me; a nice photo and bio, a dating CV no one could resist. I could be open and vulnerable when we got chatting or on the first date. I thought the simple part was matching or swiping right or left, and I didn't bother reading a profile until someone matched with me or stood out. I didn't have the time or money to spend getting to know most of them anyway. I thought it would be easy, but it wasn't.

I struggled. The women I was attracted to often showed no interest in me, while those who were interested didn't meet my needs; usually being too old and not wanting kids or not on the same wavelength. To increase my chances, I decided to change my approach. First, I adjusted my profile to claim I was ten years younger while stating my real age in my bio. This trick helped me attract more women under 40, who typically set filters below 50. Although I felt uneasy about lying, it worked, and when questioned, most women didn't mind as I looked younger. Secondly, I needed a way to stand out and initiate conversations with the most sought-after women. I began commenting on their bios to spark discussions. However, managing multiple conversations became challenging when trying to identify genuine compatibility.

The Circus Question

That's when I had my lightbulb moment: I needed an engaging opening question that would capture attention and prompt a response. It had to reveal something meaningful about the person, including their personality and ideal relationship dynamic. I was a fan of Myers-Briggs personality tests, but asking someone to take one isn't exactly a fun opener. I wanted an opening line that was simple, fun, and offered varied choices, allowing people to express themselves easily without needing to ask a question back. My initial idea was to think of a scenario where diverse relationship dynamics coexisted under one roof.

Eureka! The circus analogy was born. The circus is perfect as it encompasses a variety of characters and relationship dynamics; acts and performers literally working in harmony. The analogy for perfect harmony in my own relationship dynamic was what I was seeking. I asked myself what I would be if I were in a circus. The answer was obvious: The Ringmaster. Why? Because I was confident, loved being in control, enjoyed organising people, sought admiration, was flamboyant and diplomatic, charming, and loved to entertain. I preferred to lead my relationships, enjoying a partner who would challenge me while respecting that, in times of need, they could rely on me. But, as I mentioned, I preferred things my way.

I devised my Circus Question to be very simple. It has evolved over time and now works surprisingly well. It consists of two parts. The first part asks you to imagine the location, tapping into the conscious mind to create a familiar setting. The second part taps into the unconscious mind, presenting an opportunity to associate with a role that identifies your ideal dynamic. Within a circus, there are relationships that exist in harmony, as a spectrum of power dynamics and polarities. Two obvious examples; at opposite ends of the spectrum sit The Lion Tamer, who exerts complete control over their obedient lions; an imbalanced power dynamic exists between them. In the middle of the spectrum sits The Flying Trapeze act, where the Catcher and the Flyer swing in unity, sharing a more balanced power dynamic. While the analogy isn't foolproof, it serves as a good indicator for compatibility. It's an even greater tool to identify whom to avoid.

Interestingly, I've never had a specific type; all my past relationships formed a rich tapestry of different women. I have always been drawn to personality, intellect as much as physical appearance. Ideally, someone pretty, slim, with a nice figure; it didn't matter if they were blonde, brunette, or redhead, as long as they had something about them; someone loving, affectionate, caring, and with a sense of humour to match mine.

So, who would be my ideal match in a circus? The Ringmaster's matches were varied, but as I would discover, any of the balanced acts worked better than the imbalanced ones where there was conflict. This was perhaps where I had issues in the past where I was constantly trying to make the dynamic work, pushing a square peg into a round hole as it were, trying to mould my partner into someone who I wanted them to be. It was never going to work.

My dating game changed. Using the Circus Question as an opener garnered a multitude of interesting responses. Women were inspired to reply with full descriptions of their imagined scenarios and why. It didn't take long for me to realise that my ideal dynamic would be with someone more balanced but still wanting to be led. I found that speaking to women who chose the role of Lion Tamer often clashed with me; they wanted to control and lead me, which never worked. Likewise, I met a few lions who wanted to be completely controlled, and they weren't challenging enough for me. What I learned was that every role was perfect for someone; there wasn't a good or bad choice; just what was right for you!

I was able to filter my matches based on their answers. I became ruthless; if it wasn't a match, I was polite yet firm. I began explaining why we wouldn't be compatible due to our conflicting dynamics. Most were fascinated and took my comments on board, allowing me to coach them in their quest for a good match and an even greater date. My workload grew, but I enjoyed it and became obsessed. It became a labour of love; hundreds of "clients" over three years, mostly Americans, with our chats often occurring throughout the night. I survived on little sleep and no pay, but the satisfaction I derived from enhancing their dating strategies was immense.

I met my wife using the same strategy. My Circus Question played a significant role in fostering our initial attraction. She embodied both the Solo Trapeze and Contortionist roles; we were compatible due to her balanced dynamic, relying on trust and confidence while still being led. Our relationship deepened; we moved in together and later married. My wife Lucy, who is my rock, has allowed me to flourish, just as I hope I have for her. She's a truly amazing woman. Two years into our relationship, I was diagnosed with Crohn's disease. It's not clear if my Crohn's was due to the stress I'd inflicted on my body over the years, but it does trigger flare-ups and throws my whole ecosystem off balance. It's one of those illnesses that you can't see, but it certainly impacts your day-to-day life. Having an understanding and patient partner is crucial.

I'm grateful and fortunate to have Lucy's support in my life. While our relationship is imperfectly perfect, we've learned to compromise on matters that are minor in the grander scheme of things. We now have three beautiful and healthy children under six years old; every day is a blessing, and even though it can be tough, it puts a smile on my face, and I wouldn't have it any other way.

My coaching business didn't really get off the ground, as I had less time to devote to my clients. Even though I had begun charging, it hadn't yet grown into a business that could sustain a real livelihood, as most of my paying clients weren't in my time zone. So, I focused on working as a Project Manager in the construction industry and took over Dad's business when he retired; something I enjoyed but wasn't as passionate about. Having a young family solidified the need for a regular income, and that was that; until recently.

Courage Doesn't Wait for Anyone, But You

And here we are, I've decided to start helping people again, primarily women over the age of 30, especially those who have almost given up on dating. Whilst I enjoy one to one, with the growth of online group coaching and apps, I believe I can reach more people more easily, and my work will be time-friendly, allowing me to spend quality time with my young family while helping others in need.

Inspiring others to find love and realise their own relationship potential through informed choices and a clear strategy is something I truly wish to do. My goal is to educate as many people as possible about the crucial role dynamics play in healthy relationships. "Toxic" and "Narcissist" are now relationship buzzwords that send shivers down the spine of every page in social media. I want to share my system and strategy to help women avoid this negativity. Women like you are more open to transformation and change. I want to educate so it may be passed down to our children, and future generations may form loving, lasting relationships that flourish and are free of trauma, where possible. It's a tall ask, but if we all do our bit, they will have us to thank.

So don't you give up on your dream of finding love and realising your potential. I want to teach you how to take control, date with confidence, avoid toxicity, make better choices, get what you need, and date with a smile again. There isn't enough space to explain everything here, but if you're interested in learning more about my work and how it can get you the results you want and provide the rewards I've experienced and shared with others, please feel free to investigate further by visiting my website or social media pages for more information.

Now, what about your own answer to my Circus Question? Well, you can visit my website and upload it there, and I will endeavour to send you a reply and details about my forthcoming book and App, "The Circus Question," which will give you that edge while dating!

I promise you that your dating strategy will never be the same again!

Andreas

Website: www.relationshipdynamics.online

Facebook: www.facebook.com/andreasdatingcoach.1/

CHAPTER 11

Breaking Free from Darkness:

A Path to Mental Wellness and Hope

By Nezha Ait Akka

Empowerment Coach for Overwhelmed Women

Where It All Began: My Journey's Initial Challenges

Imagine you're going about your day, working or looking after your children, or you're sleeping in your bed, and then suddenly, without warning, you're overcome by an intense surge of fear and anxiety. Physically, your heart starts racing uncontrollably, as if trying to escape your chest, while your breathing becomes rapid and shallow, making it feel like you can't get enough air, and you are dying. Your muscles tense up, and you might feel shaky and jittery, as if you're preparing to face an imminent danger. These physical feelings are so extreme that you can't fathom what's happening to you. You don't realise that there is no condition that poses a threat to your safety, health, or well-being, and at the same time your body is signalling there is a grave danger! It's insane, you keep looking out for the danger but there is NO danger.

Emotionally, it's like being caught in a storm of overwhelming dread and panic. Thoughts rush through your mind at lightning speed, often irrational and catastrophic, despite your rational understanding that there's no immediate threat. It's as if your mind has hit a panic button, flooding your whole system with adrenaline and cortisol hormones, and pushing you into fight-or-flight mode, even in the absence of any real danger. You try to calm your emotions, but nothing works at first, people around you tell you to calm down, that nothing is going to happen to you, yet the strong feelings you feel are so powerful that they take away your reasoning abilities to deal with the attacks. It feels like you suddenly get all the feelings we can feel during a whole day in a few seconds and each one of them is getting more intense than the other ones.

Psychologically, a panic attack can be profoundly disorienting and isolating. The experience can disrupt your sense of reality, making time seem to stretch or compress unpredictably. You might feel detached from yourself or your surroundings, creating a sense of unreality or dissociation. This mental detachment can leave you feeling as though you're observing events from a distance, heightening the sense of isolation and loneliness.

The intense fear and anxiety during a panic attack is overwhelming, and even after the physical symptoms have subsided, the psychological effects can linger. You may feel emotionally drained, with heightened sensitivity to stress and a persistent sense of unease. This mental exhaustion can impact your mood, concentration, and overall sense of well-being, often making it difficult to return to a state of normality. The shame you feel surrounding your mental state can significantly amplify your stress levels. When you feel embarrassed or guilty about your emotional struggles, it creates an additional layer of pressure and self-judgement. This heightened self-criticism only exacerbates your stress, making it harder to manage and overcome. Recognising that these feelings of shame contribute to your stress is a crucial step towards addressing both your mental health and overall well-being.

Let me tell you my story about my life-long struggles

I remember how anxious I was as a child. At the time, I couldn't fully understand it, but looking back, I now see the signs of ADHD coupled with severe anxiety. I struggled with nail-biting, fidgeting, and daydreaming in class. Every noise and movement in the classroom felt overwhelming. I often found it hard to follow instructions and remember the exercises, even though I was a good student. My drive to excel was fuelled by my own pressure to remember my lessons, which led to perfectionism and intense frustration when things didn't go as planned. I was an overthinker, constantly over analysing every little detail of what

I was going to do, say, eat, where I was going, and how I would behave in different situations. I know most of us naturally think about these things, but for me, it consumed so much energy and mental space that I ended up obsessing over countless ways things could go wrong.

This behaviour caught up with me and I started feeling panic attacks by 16 or 17 years old.

Normal situations were overwhelming, frightening, and I felt scared most of the time. I was so self-conscious that other people could see how I was feeling inside that I tried to hide it with make-up, attitude, outgoing and rebellious behaviours. I felt isolated and lonely.

Shame was a part of my life from childhood and stayed with me well into my adult life. Life as a teen was hard, my hormones were so imbalanced I spent the first few days of my periods in bed. It also affected my mood and mental health as I felt low for a few days a month.

I didn't tell my parents much about how I felt nor my struggles, although they could see I was grumpy, irritable, moody. I'm sure they put everything down to the adolescence stages. I sought some help and started taking some anti-anxiety medication and some sleeping tablets.

By the time I turned 20, my panic attacks had become both more frequent and more severe. The intensity of the episodes left me feeling overwhelmed and unable to manage daily responsibilities effectively. My emotional stability deteriorated, making it increasingly difficult to focus on my studies and keep up with work commitments. The persistent anxiety and frequent panic attacks disrupted my ability to maintain a consistent routine, leading to significant challenges in balancing academic and professional demands. This period marked a significant struggle as I grappled with the escalating impact of my mental health on my overall functioning and daily life.

At times, I tried to over-control my life, hoping to reduce the attacks, but they were overwhelming, leaving me powerless to manage them. They would strike unexpectedly while I was sitting, eating, walking, or sleeping. There was no clear pattern to identify or control them—they were simply controlling me.

Shame was a constant presence in my life, affecting every aspect of my daily existence. It was not just a brief emotion but a deeply ingrained force that shaped my interactions and self-perception. The weight of this shame made it difficult for me to be open about my struggles, leading me to hide my feelings as a means of coping. Masking my true emotions provided a temporary sense of comfort and safety, allowing me to maintain a facade of normality in social and professional settings. This disguise, however, also meant I missed out on the opportunity to seek support and understanding, further deepening my sense of isolation and internal conflict. I spent years consumed by guilt, shame, and anxiety, struggling to finish anything I started.

The Turning Point: What Led Me to Embrace Healing

At the age of 27, I had my first son prematurely due to incredibly early contractions. Motherhood was and still is a profound journey that transforms every aspect of my life. It encompasses a wide range of experiences, from the joy of first smiles to the challenges of sleepless nights. It demands patience, resilience, and boundless love, as mothers navigate the complexities of nurturing and guiding their children. Motherhood often brings a deep sense of purpose and fulfilment, as each day presents new opportunities to grow and bond with a child. Personally, it is a journey of continuous learning and unconditional love, shaping both me as a mother and my children in meaningful ways. As I write this chapter, my first born is 26 years old, soon to be 27.

I think because I was busy looking after my son, I was less into my head. Motherhood has this powerful boost to make you forget about yourself and swallow you whole into this state of total surrender to your child. As I was raising my son, I learned to recognise my feelings, behaviours and thoughts. I started feeling much better, motherhood felt great! Caring for my son helped me feel proud and for once a bit less ashamed about how I felt inside.

At 31, I became a new mom again, facing the challenges of difficult pregnancies with early contractions and bed rest to keep my babies safe. When my second son was born, I immediately sensed he was different. His autism diagnosis would come at three years old. I remember managing his needs and adjusting to new routines was overwhelming, yet I was under estimating the crucial need for self-care and support during that challenging period.

In 2002, we decided to move from our sunny life in Marbella to London! That was a big move with 2 little kids and not much savings, but I was confident we would make a life for us in the UK. My London lifestyle had me working long hours, commuting about two hours daily, and caring for my children. But at 32, tragedy struck my family, and within months, my panic attacks returned—severe, persistent, and relentless. My mental health deteriorated so much that I had to resign from my job in central London.

After that day, things became worse. I hated staying by myself, I was panicking all the time and daily stuff started to be difficult for me. I was panicking about having panic attacks, making me even more panicked! My worry was to be caught by strangers or people I knew and to have a meltdown in front of them. I was self-conscious all the time and trying to hide my state of mind, always checking that I was acting accordingly to the situations I was in, looking for anyone noticing my anxiety, and getting even more anxious. It was exhausting. Panic attacks were exhausting. I felt trapped.

During that time, I knew I needed help. I wanted to feel better, healthier, happier, and free from these attacks. The hardest part was seeking help. My anxious state felt like a prison, and I wasn't sure how to escape it. Even the thought of getting help was daunting because it meant risking that people would find out about my secret.

This fear of being exposed keeps many mental health sufferers from reaching out. But I had reached a point where I couldn't function, and I wanted to be a great mom for my children. They were too important to me, so I opened up about my intentions and began searching for a therapist.

The Moment I Realised I Needed Therapy

What made me finally decide to seek therapy? I desperately wanted to get better. The only things on my mind every day were stopping my panic attacks and finding a way to feel better. Deep down, I knew there was another version of myself waiting to emerge—a version that wasn't defined by fear and anxiety. I believed that what I was going through was temporary, not permanent, and that I could overcome it.

I know many people don't seek help and suffer in silence. The shame and despair only deepen their mental health struggles. Anxiety is a constant battle with overwhelming fears and worries that feel impossible to control. It's like living on edge, always bracing for something bad to happen. The physical symptoms—like a racing heart, trembling, and shortness of breath—can be relentless. Wherever you go, you can't stop imagining scenarios that might trigger a panic attack. It's exhausting. I remember feeling like prey in a jungle of invisible dangers, trapped by my own mind.

For years, I thought of myself as an anxious person with something fundamentally wrong with her. I felt like an imposter, pretending to be a mother in control when, inside, everything was chaos. I became skilled at hiding my struggles, but it was draining. Only my close family knew a little of what I was going through, but I avoided burdening them with the full truth.

The tipping point came when I became afraid to leave my house, fearing panic attacks in public, especially in front of my kids. I recall one day when my ex and I were travelling by train with our two sons. As we stood on the platform, I felt a panic attack building, and nothing could calm me down. When the train arrived, I suddenly stopped and insisted we wait for the next one. I felt terrible as we waited for one or two more trains to pass before I could manage to get on. The shame and guilt were overwhelming. My ex was supportive, but I wasn't proud of myself.

After a panic attack, it's like you've been running from a lion, even though you've been standing still. Your body feels shattered, and your mind is flooded with adrenaline and cortisol. The physical and emotional aftermath is draining, leaving you exhausted.

Eventually, I reached a point where I couldn't even take the kids to school. I stayed indoors most of the time, only feeling safe within the confines of my home. I knew this wasn't fair to myself, my children, or my family. I couldn't live like this anymore, so I decided to seek therapy.

I was terrified of my uncontrollable panic attacks, so finding the right therapist was crucial. Within a few days, I connected with a woman who seemed to understand. In our initial phone session, I shared my struggles with anxiety, panic attacks, a family tragedy, and parts of my childhood. She listened with genuine compassion, explaining how anxiety works and how panic attacks are triggered. By the end of the call, I felt a mix of excitement, hope, and worry about how I'd manage to get to her office for weekly sessions.

Therapy was painful and draining, forcing me to relive and rethink past agony. However, I would recommend it to anyone facing similar struggles because, without it, I wouldn't have been able to manage my anxiety. Therapy provides a safe space to explore your thoughts and emotions with a professional who listens without judgement. It gave me the tools, insights, and strategies to improve my well-being.

As we explored past events, I started to understand the roots of my anxiety and panic attacks. I learned to recognise my thought patterns, which helped reduce the frequency and intensity of my attacks. While they didn't disappear overnight, therapy taught me how to control them and manage my anxiety healthily.

After about a year, I felt much better and began exploring personal growth, how the brain works, and different methods to calm my nervous system. Understanding my triggers—like fatigue, overwhelm, or busy places—helped me manage my anxiety. Over time, I realised that anxiety is common in people with ADHD, which explained some of my struggles and marked the start of a new chapter in my life.

Professionally, after the bad experience of being an employee, I knew I wanted to be independent and work for myself. I became self-employed and grew my little family business importing Moroccan handicraft to London! Thinking about it, it was the best decision for my family! Within a year or so, I then went to collaborate in a Moroccan Restaurant in one of the most visited areas of London, the Stables in Camden Market. Life was busy!

How My Journey Shaped My Life and Business Success

I'm at the airport, whilst waiting for my flight, writing this chapter. Just a few years ago, I never would have imagined I'd be flying again. I remember how often I wanted to go out, to do so many activities with the kids, but I was always anxious about what could go wrong. So many times, I overthought the worst-case scenarios, stopping myself from living a normal life, from taking the kids on holidays, and truly enjoying life. Don't get me wrong—my kids had plenty of weekly activities like football, Arabic classes, swimming, kickboxing, and gymnastics. We also attended regular therapies for their special needs—speech therapy, occupational therapy, cranial osteopathy, psychologists... And there were always playgroups, park outings, school trips, birthday parties, and meals out. I managed it all for years, with anxiety as my constant companion, always sitting front and centre.

Growing my business and working most days, with an unstable mental health was challenging, but we are so used to pushing through that it almost seemed normal.

Anxiety is incredibly challenging because it dictates how you live your life. I often had to improvise on the spot, waking up each morning to gauge my state of mind before planning anything. I would inevitably overthink all the things that could go wrong, which often led to me holding back from doing what I wanted.

So, I kept things to the bare minimum—taking care of the kids and their activities, cooking, and managing my business. I was on autopilot the whole time, with no mental space left to think about anything beyond my daily responsibilities. With anxiety like that, your mind becomes so overloaded with worries that there's no room left for rest, hobbies, fun…

That's how living with anxiety really held me back, and I would say it stole many years of happiness and joy from my life.

I'm not sure I can get those lost years back, but that's not the purpose of sharing my experience. My goal is to help at least one person struggling with anxiety and show them that there is light at the end of the tunnel—opportunities for healing, well-being, and health.

Don't let anxiety control your life or give it all your power. The more you focus on it, the more powerful it becomes. It's like a plant: the more you water and feed it, the more it grows. The more you dwell on your anxiety, the more anxious you become.

It may sound odd, but I grew accustomed to my anxious state. It became a familiar, daily presence—normal to some extent, though never completely comfortable.

Resilience Through Self-Care – How Prioritising Mental Health Shaped My Journey

Resilience. My old state of mind taught me resilience.

I learned to become resilient. Think about it, every day I suffered with anxiety, I learned something from it. Every panic attack was a sign for me to deal with something in my life. All these anxiety moments were my body and mind trying to connect and work together for my well being.

Reflecting on my journey through anxiety, the pivotal change came when I prioritised my mental health and self-care. I once felt overwhelmed by fear and self-doubt, convinced my struggles would never end. But focusing on self-care sparked my transformation.

Imagine being stuck in a cycle where each day feels like a battle. That was my reality until I realised surviving wasn't enough—I needed to thrive. Seeking help through therapy was crucial. Each session was a step toward understanding and managing my anxiety better.

Alongside therapy, I made self-care a core part of my recovery. I embraced it as an essential practice rather than an occasional indulgence. I explored various methods, from cognitive behavioural therapy, lifestyle changes to essential oils and coaching. Each approach contributed to my well-being, helping me manage stress and build resilience.

What I discovered was transformative: taking care of my mental health was about creating a nurturing lifestyle for my whole being—whether as a woman, mother, or entrepreneur. Self-care became my anchor, providing strength to face challenges and maintain balance.

To anyone struggling with anxiety or mental health issues, prioritise your mental health and self-care. It's not just about managing symptoms; it's about creating a supportive environment. Embrace therapy, explore self-care practices, and focus on your well-being.

Resilience grows from self-care. By nurturing your mental health, you build a foundation of strength to navigate life's ups and downs. By taking care of yourself, you pave the way for a stronger, empowered you.

Here are my **go-to tips** for calming down when anxiety strikes, and when you are worried about a panic attack. These methods have really worked for me, and I encourage you to give them a try:

Always Carrying a Cold-Water Bottle: I never leave home without a cold-water bottle. When I sense a panic attack coming on, I take a few sips or splash some on my face. The cold sensation jolts me out of my spiralling thoughts and anchors me in the present moment.

Using Rescue Remedy herbal flowers: I always keep a little bottle of Rescue Remedy in my handbag. When anxiety starts creeping in, I take a few drops. It's amazing how focusing on this simple action helps me ground myself and shift my mind away from anxiety.

Grounding with Simple Anchoring Techniques: Since becoming a coach and NLP practitioner, I've found grounding myself with small anchoring techniques to be incredibly effective. Whether it's pressing my fingers together or giving myself a self-hug, these little actions help me regain control and calm down quickly.

Our mental health often signals what we need to address. Even in crises, listening to these signals and seeking resources can lead to healing. My mission is to help others because I once found transformation through support. Has my anxiety vanished entirely? No. But I can control it, and it no longer prevents me from travelling, working, growing personally, or making plans. If I can do it, so can you!

I never imagined I'd share my story, especially one I once viewed as shameful. However, when the opportunity arose to write about it for

World Mental Health Day, I embraced it wholeheartedly. I saw it as a chance to contribute to a meaningful cause and offer hope to others. Perhaps my story will inspire one of you to share your own journey, creating a ripple effect that touches and uplifts many.

These days, when I'm not strolling through nature in my local park or sharing empowering content on my social media platforms, you'll find me helping overwhelmed women reclaim their balance, boost their self-care, and navigate their stress. I guide them in rediscovering their strength, building resilience, and prioritising their well-being—ultimately leading them to more fulfilling and empowered lives.

If my story speaks to you or if you need support, let's connect.

Get in touch with Nezha here: www.snipfeed.co/nezha —your voice matters, and together, we can build a supportive community.

CHAPTER 12

By Nina McLeod

Advanced Life Coach & Mentor,

Meditation Teacher & Somatic Therapist

Suck It Up Sister

As an 80s child, people didn't talk about mental health or wellbeing at all. If you misbehaved, you were labelled a delinquent, from a bad family, uneducated, outright naughty, and judged heavily. It was never considered that you may be neurodiverse nor were you ever asked, "What happened to you?" If you appeared to have mental health issues as an adult, then there was clearly something wrong with you, and then attached the stigma.

With more compassion, empathy, and understanding nowadays, while some views and opinions stay unchanged, as a society we have up-levelled.

Rarely visiting a doctor unless needing my tonsils removed, or a repair on my cracked skull when young, I haven't accumulated certain labels for my life's journey thus far. Deciding to collaborate on this book and choosing which part of my challenging life to share was difficult. But in that decision-making, I realised I had been undiagnosed with multiple mental health challenges for many years.

For this book I'm going to start at age 18, it was then that I felt extremely off balance and unwell in my mind. I decided to visit the GP, not feeling like myself. I was blushing easily at work, a very male-dominated environment where I was preyed upon, naive, gullible, vulnerable, open, and honest. I naturally see the best in others and have a history of excusing unacceptable behaviour.

Daily events included being whistled at, called out, asked out (even though I had a boyfriend), faced with inappropriate suggestions, boundary violations, gentle touches, and more. Today, this would be seen as sexual harassment, but in the 90s, I had to "suck it up," say nothing, complain to nobody because nobody would care, listen, or believe me. Or was that just my learned behaviour with my inaccurate perception of the world?

By this point, I had already left home at 17 due to constant bickering with Mum, moving in with my boyfriend, a young soldier. Our relationship was filled with fun, laughter and excitement, drinking in pubs at 16, (yes 16) dancing, and living life. But when he left the army to be with me, things changed. He was used to banter and mick-taking with young soldiers. I needed connection, gentleness, and kindness after the life I had led up to this point.

When this domineering, stubborn, arrogant, and even aggressive man shared my home, and work was also dominated by masculinity, my spirit broke. My beliefs evolved into negative perceptions about myself I had never thought to be true.

By then, I had gone through a lot, (a story for another time) but I couldn't manage the mental and emotional challenges any longer. They were making me physically ill. I have always believed in the metaphysical anatomy, that our emotions genuinely make us physically ill if left unaware or hidden. I was experiencing a bad back, frequent blushing (aggravated by men at work), irregular breathing, bad dreams, disturbed sleep, and IBS. My identity as lively, fun, and loving was now lost and broken.

Anxiety, Breakdown, Restart

When I finally reached out after enduring so much and staying silent for years, the GP diagnosed me with anxiety. I was told to take time off work and prescribed medication. Although I accepted the anxiety diagnosis, it was clear it was much more than that. She had run through a checklist, likely akin to the GAD-7 form used today, and I wasn't asked any deep and meaningful questions to discover what was hidden within and why.

I walked out to my mum who was waiting outside and broke down in tears. It was at that moment I realised I really wasn't OK and that what I had been experiencing daily wasn't OK either. Oh and I refused the medication!

I'd never known anyone to take medication for anything other than physical aches and pains, so it didn't make sense to me. Even at 18, I knew that medication for the mind wasn't the right way forward for me.

I had to accept this breakdown as a way out of the life I had been accepting and simply putting up with, to create a change and take control of my present and future for my mind, body, and soul survival. I quit my job, I broke up with my boyfriend and I moved back home with my mum and brother again. It wasn't easy, but I did it. My relationship with Mum was easier now, I guess Mum knew that I needed her, and I knew this too.

For work, I turned to home care. I looked after mentally ill clients, neurodivergent individuals (although this wasn't named that then), and the elderly. From PTSD, schizophrenia, bipolar disorder, eating disorders, cancer patients, ME, and physically disabled individuals, to the lovely old folk with little to no family support.

Once again, despite my younger years below age 18 remaining unshared, I found myself caring for others: being their go-to, lean-on, advocate, ally, carer, and confidant.

I loved it but gave it my all. I worked seven days a week, allowing clients my number for emergencies. And yes, they used it; once at midnight when the carer after me had connected the catheter inaccurately and the frantic wife needed help with her husband. Of course, I went. I dedicated my time and energy to genuinely caring for each of my clients. I love people—their uniqueness, their stories, their lives—and helping to improve it for them.

Unsurprisingly, after giving my heart and soul, I reached what we'd now call burnout, but I named it "Cared Out." Did you know that 1 in 4 people in the UK experience mental health issues each year, and 1 in 6 report common issues like anxiety and depression daily?

Once more, I quit my job, never worrying about the next one. However, this time I packed all my belongings into my black Ford Orion which I became a professional at jumpstarting alone and moved to the North of England where I had family, all within a few days.

Wey Aye, You're A Roar Man

What I didn't foresee was what awaited me there. I'm sorry to say this is a story for another day. However, I will share that the person I stayed with was family and someone I loved. She was older, someone I had always admired, yet I found her in the worst state ever—psychologically, emotionally, physically, and socially.

I became the carer again, as I always had, without complaints. It was a pattern, a behaviour, a comfort without comfort perhaps that I knew well. I knew how to be strong for others, how to take care of them, make them happy, make them laugh, say yes, all the time, keep my voice quiet, empower them to believe in themselves and strive for more in their lives, or simply accept with compassion where they are. Oh, and within a few weeks, I had started working in a severe dementia home with some very aggressive patients, being only 18 years old this was very insightful, even frightening at times.

One day, I drove my family member and her friend to see a Clairvoyant. I had booked a slot too, yet intuitively I knew I wouldn't have it done. When my turn came, the Clairvoyant proclaimed she was too tired. I accepted this and decided to trust my intuition for what I needed to know.

This was a turning point—a moment of Epiphany. I woke up within the next few days and decided to travel back 334 miles to my hometown as quickly as I had decided to travel to north Tyneside. The grass wasn't greener. I wasn't free or independent, and I couldn't escape this caring role my life seemed set on for me. The 60's scene of drugs, crime, and parties was closing in on me, I had to take control of my life because no one was coming to save me.

Intuitively, I felt something would happen with me and a car, so I was very mindful on the 7-hour drive back south, blaring 'LeAnn Rimes - Can't Fight the Moonlight,' driver's window wound down, north winds blowing my hair and freezing my face to prevent me from falling asleep as snow still lay on the roadside. Did I mention both times I left it was at night? Little traffic, just cruising with the deep blue night sky, peaceful, and feeling free.

So focused on those elements of my journey I took a wrong turn and ended up in central London on a Saturday night. That was fun, genuinely it was, I had never been to London. Even though I wasn't sightseeing, and it was gridlocked, I witnessed people walking all over the roads, in groups of fancy dress or glamour having fun and being who they had chosen to be.

With no sat nav, just good ole' written directions or a map I rarely used, I had thought if I could get to the north of England originally, then I could get back to the south of England. Not considering the roads, directions, and signs were completely different. No logic in my thinking!

Face Your Fears or Freeze

Remember the intuition and concern I had about something happening to me and a car? I arrived home safely, but I experienced two life-changing incidents. For the nature of this story, I will share one. It was a serious car accident while I was seated in the back. The driver, a young man in his early 20s was showing off, testing his car's speed. Travelling around 100 mph, he lost control after travelling over a known hump in the road. Thankfully, we didn't flip, but we ended up in a field after hitting the verges on both sides of the road multiple times and leaving skid marks that lasted over a year.

I recall him screaming "F#*? *F#*?*" repeatedly as he struggled to control the vehicle. It was terrifying yet it all happened so fast. My back pressed against the car's ceiling, and I couldn't open the door when the car finally stopped. He was crying, saying, "I shouldn't have been driving like that with you in the car, I'm so sorry." All I could do was reassure him, my usual, "It's OK, I'm OK."

That night at my mum's, I realised I wasn't OK. I went into shock in my bedroom. My entire life flashed before me, reliving what happened and contemplating what could have happened. I was grateful to be alive, but the scene kept playing in my mind. I couldn't sleep, stop crying, or stop trembling. After that experience, I couldn't get into a car for months, couldn't travel that road, or talk about it. I disconnected from the driver and was displaying a classic case of PTSD.

My Dad, a soldier and driver in the army who had served all over the world, wanted me to get over it for my well-being. He believed in what I now know to be exposure therapy.

Dad put me in his car. I didn't argue, I respected and trusted him. Unbeknownst to me, he intended to drive insanely fast and risky, even overtaking an HGV uphill at great speed without me as a passenger being able to see if it was clear. Dad wanted to show me that a good driver could drive fast and be safe and that I needed to trust again. I was scared, angry, and crying, but still, I trusted. Oddly enough, it worked!

Looking back, it was the right thing to do for me. That experience, as terrifying as it was, helped me overcome my fear and trust again. Do you have a similar experience when facing a fear head-on made a significant difference?

Desperately Seeking... Self

I have countless life stories to share, but only one chapter in this book. If you're keen on hearing more, maybe an entire book, just let me know!

Perhaps you're 'Desperately Seeking Nina' as I was, and a little nod to the 80's classic movie "Desperately Seeking Susan "starring Madonna.

My two children call me a boomer, a label I've never accepted because I feel young at heart. I genuinely forget my age because it's just a number, but maybe they're right about some things and how I've chosen to reflect on the past in my style of writing.

Everything I've grown through has shown me that my life's pathway and purpose, whether joyous or challenging, is to care for others, to support, encourage, guide, and believe in them and their stories. It's about helping them live their best lives, knowing authentically that this 'best life' ideal, varies from person to person.

No matter what challenges I've faced, physically, emotionally, or with my mental health - I didn't choose to lean on medication. I'm not suggesting this path is for everyone; it's important to decide what's right for you. But I believe I'm here for an important reason and a bigger purpose.

When I was at death's door twice due to my physical health, it was intravenous medication that saved me. Acute trauma often needs medical intervention. However, one life-threatening illness I had when my firstborn was only five weeks old was caused by the medication I was taking to improve symptoms of a previously diagnosed dis-ease, and one that took my dear nan from us several years later.

I spent my first Mother's Day in the hospital, fighting for my life physically and struggling with rejection and upset emotionally, because my son seemed happy enough without me and was being cared for by my mum. I didn't want to see either of them because it hurt. These feelings of anger, frustration, hurt, and sadness were misguided and unfairly directed at my mum, who was kindly caring for my baby out of love for us both. This is an example of a new mum experiencing mental health problems, which can manifest in various ways at any time.

I strongly believe that our bodies speak to us, our mind plays tricks on us, and our souls celebrate us. Especially when we listen and take action to help ourselves. This belief has helped guide me through my experiences and kept me focused on my life's purpose.

Have you also found that listening to yourself and taking action has helped you overcome personal challenges?

Save Yourself, No-One Is Coming

Over the last 21 years, I've trained in various fields, all aimed at helping others so they can help themselves. But that journey had to start with me. Oh, my goodness, it was hard. To actually look at myself, take care of myself, and dive deep into everything - to forgive, accept, allow, love, release, and let go of anything that wasn't serving me positively.

Everything I've learned, I've taken myself through, and I still do this today. For me, this is how it should be. I haven't only learned from textbooks or pre-recorded training. Sure, I've had some great takeaways from fantastic books and courses, but my experience, empathy, and integrity are lived, learned, embodied, and congruent. It's been painful and exciting, not to mention blooming expensive!

I specialise now in helping intuitive women navigate mental health challenges holistically without medication. I've worked with hundreds of women ranging from 17 to their late 70s, with symptoms and stories that are sometimes similar and completely different.

Why have I chosen this? Because I have lived experience and am educated. I believe so many women have learned to stay quiet, stay small, put up with what they don't want, and are stuck in fear of judgement, loneliness, abuse, not being good enough, comparison, and not being respected, heard, seen, or believed.

So many, like me, have experienced or are still experiencing manipulation, trauma, abuse, judgement, PTSD, grief, loss, anxiety, stress, OCD, eating disorders, panic attacks, phobias, overwhelm, burnout, identity crises, separation/divorce, neurodiversity, and sadly, the list goes on.

What's more, I am a woman. I am still young, I have been a younger woman, a young girl, a toddler, and a baby. I know, can you imagine that? What a cute baby I was too. I am most certainly an old soul, capable of collaborating with all women, meeting them exactly where they are in their lives, and navigating a clear pathway to where they want to be instead.

The NHS is overwhelmed, private practices are now busy, and medication is their go-to because that is how they've been trained, not dismissing how desperately they're needed. I respect them and those who have chosen auxiliary roles in the medical profession. In July 2024, I walked a 10K fundraiser for our local hospital with my eldest son, in memory of my dad, his granddad, who lost his fight to cancer. The medical staff there were amazing and are very much needed.

But here's the thing - over 86 million antidepressants and more than 8.6 million people were identified in 2023/24, with four of the five groups of drugs being prescribed most often in the most deprived areas. This to me is absolute madness. Records state medications don't cure mental health conditions. They can make your symptoms and feelings go away or lessen, but if you stop taking them, your symptoms may come back.

Remember, your journey to self-care starts with you. Have you found ways to start taking care of yourself that have made a difference?

Brain Power Assisted Bravery

The thoughts in your mind, the stories you hear, the patterns and behaviours you witness in yourself, YOU can change. Most of our stories, experiences, situations, relationships, reactions, and triggers aren't the ones we chose. We may think we did, but it's programming - our core beliefs, learned behaviours, and the unconscious mind wanting to keep us safe. This programming attempts to keep us safe yet stuck, protecting us from feeling uncertain, afraid, fearful, sad, rejected, neglected, unwanted, not enough, unloved, and unworthy; and yet that's exactly what we become.

Neuroscience has been fantastic for coaches and mentors, defining and explaining in simple terms what we already knew but is now backed by science. Neuroplasticity is the brain's ability to reorganise itself by forming new neural pathways throughout life and in response to experiences. While the brain usually does this in response to injury, trauma, or disease, humans can slowly rewire these pathways themselves by focusing their attention. "Neurons that wire together fire together," creating new pathways, deprogramming, and reprogramming of your choosing, which is outstanding!

What? I hear you shout... Yes, this is true. So, what are you waiting for? The old self wants to stay where it is, even if it's not comfortable or fun. It's a known place, and that's safe and easier than trying to change. We need to remind ourselves that no one is coming to save us, we must take control and save ourselves.

This will be different for each of us, naturally. When working with my clients, I combine what some call a little "woo-woo" (Energetics, Kinesiology, EFT, Breathwork, Hypnotherapy, Mindfulness, Inner-child healing, Somatic, Law of Attraction, and Sound therapy) with evidence-based studies (NLP, Coaching, Counselling, Mental Health, Psychology, CBT, Meditation, Mindfulness, Somatic Therapy for Complex Traumas) to name a few.

I hope that my chapter in this amazing book has inspired you to take control of your life in a way that perhaps you hadn't thought of before. Remember, the past is just a memory, the future isn't yet written, and we only have this present moment, right here, right now.

Do not allow the judgement of the past, or the fear of the future to define your presence.

It is Your Life, Your Decision, Your Body, Your Mind, Your Soul, Live Life by Your Design!

Remember: "If You Always Do What You've Always Done, You'll Always Get What You've Always Got." **~ Henry Ford**

Please accept my gift and let's connect—from my soul to yours:

Linktree: www.linktr.ee/Nina.McLeod_Coach.and.Mentor

COURAGE

"COURAGE, ABOVE ALL THINGS, IS THE FIRST QUALITY OF A WARRIOR."

- CARL VON CLAUSEWITZ

CHAPTER 13

From Darkness to Light: A Mother's Journey Through Mental Health and Healing

By Noor Aishah

The Unexpected Journey Begins

In 2016, our family's life was turned upside down. My son, once vibrant and outgoing, began refusing to attend school in Secondary Three (at 15 years old). Initially, we dismissed it as typical teenage rebellion, but reality soon shattered our complacency.

This was a child who had always regaled us with tales from his school day, his eyes alight with enthusiasm. Soccer was his passion, and he had a close-knit group of friends. I had often mused that his gift for persuasion might lead him to become a lawyer or even a motivational speaker. But at 15, a veil of silence descended. His zest for life seemed to evaporate overnight.

Desperate to help, I took a six-month sabbatical from work. I had been advised he needed my attention, but the improvement in his attendance was fleeting at best. He struggled to rise in the mornings, preferring instead to cycle alone under the cover of darkness. Later, he confided that these nocturnal excursions were his "thinking time."

My husband and I felt lost and confused. We did not know much about mental health issues at that time and were not sure how to help our son. This was the start of a journey that would test us, change us, and eventually help us understand and care for each other better.

In hindsight, the warning signs were there, camouflaged by our own expectations. Mathematics has always been my son's Achilles' heel. As a mathematics-trained teacher, I naturally assumed the role of his tutor. But this well-intentioned support inadvertently added to his burden. He felt an immense pressure to excel in mathematics, if only to please me. Despite my assurances that his best effort was enough, his academic struggles steadily eroded his self-esteem. His Mother's Day and birthday messages often concluded with promises to improve in mathematics, each one piercing my heart deeply. My attempts to lower his expectations fell on ears deafened by his self-doubt.

The true gravity of the situation hit home in early 2019. A disturbing message from our son, accompanied by a dark meme, jolted us out of our complacency. We finally grasped that our child was grappling with something far more serious than we had imagined. After weeks of gentle coaxing, he agreed to seek medical help. This marked our family's first tentative steps into the realm of mental health care.

***Sometimes the hardest part of the journey is believing you're worthy of the trip.* - Glenn Beck**

Braving the Storms of Mental Health

Our journey to find appropriate help for our son was fraught with challenges. Faced with long waiting times in the public healthcare system, we turned to a private psychiatrist. In August 2019, we received a diagnosis: Major Depressive Disorder with Anxious Distress – Moderate Severity and Dysthymia. This moment was a paradox of emotions – relief at finally having a name for our son's struggles, yet apprehension about the long road ahead.

Post-diagnosis, we saw a glimmer of improvement in our son's condition. However, we recognised the need for comprehensive care, including psychological support to build his resilience and address the root causes of his depression. Just as we were finding our footing, the Covid-19 pandemic struck, initially showing some positive signs but ultimately worsening his condition. Despite these setbacks, there was a silver lining – our son managed to complete his diploma studies online.

2020 brought another dramatic shift to our family landscape. Our daughter's school counsellor requested a meeting, and our world tilted again. Our perfectionist, academically driven daughter was grappling with her own mental health crisis, including suicidal ideation. Her condition, at that point, seemed even more severe than her brother's. I promptly sought a psychologist for a diagnosis, and upon receiving it, I momentarily crumbled before steeling myself for her sake. The realisation that both our children were battling mental health issues was overwhelming, leaving me questioning why this was happening to our family.

We quickly learned that mental health journeys are as unique as fingerprints. Our son's recovery was a slow, undulating process with numerous setbacks and small victories. In contrast, our daughter exhibited a fierce determination to improve. For her, at her request, we adopted a holistic approach – implementing family exercise routines, increasing her therapy sessions, and exploring art therapy. Within eight months, we witnessed a remarkable transformation in her. However, the most profound change came through her spirit of volunteerism.

This period was rife with challenges. Our son's moods were volatile, often making communication difficult. There were instances of crying and even self-harm attempts to garner attention. These experiences necessitated a complete overhaul of our parenting approach. We learned the art of patient listening and the wisdom of offering less unsolicited advice. We discovered the crucial importance of creating safe spaces for our children to express themselves freely. Sometimes, this meant allowing them to text their feelings or engaging in late-night conversations when the house was quiet and calm. We even created separate chat groups for each child, recognising their distinct needs and communication styles.

***It's not about waiting for the storm to pass, it's about learning to dance in the rain.* - Vivian Greene**

Finding My Own Path to Healing

While our focus remained steadfastly on our children's well-being, my own mental health began to unravel. Anxiety and panic attacks crept into my daily life, transforming once-simple tasks into formidable challenges. Activities I once cherished became sources of dread, pushing me further into isolation.

As time progressed, my anxiety tightened its grip. It seeped into the dullest aspects of my existence, colouring every interaction and decision. In a misguided attempt to shield my son from my struggles, I retreated into silence, often shutting myself away in my room upon returning home from work. This self-imposed isolation only widened the gap between my inner turmoil and the composed facade I strived to maintain.

My battle extended beyond anxiety. Claustrophobia made crowded, confined spaces feel suffocating, while restless legs syndrome robbed me of restful sleep. Panic attacks would ambush me without warning, forcing abrupt exits from social situations and further fuelling my anxiety about future encounters.

The turning point came with the realisation that I, too, needed care. My first step towards healing was through journaling, a private outlet for my chaotic thoughts. This small act of self-care eventually led me to seek professional help. On September 1, 2023, I began my journey with medication, starting Lexapro under psychiatric care. This marked the beginning of my own path to recovery.

The transformation was noticeable. As the medication took effect, a sense of calm and control gradually returned. Tasks that had seemed insurmountable, like enduring long car rides, became achievable once more. While my recovery is an ongoing process, I have come to understand that nurturing my own mental health is crucial for supporting my children effectively.

As I continue to navigate this new landscape of self-care, I am learning to recognise the early signs of anxiety and developing coping strategies. Deep breathing exercises and grounding techniques have become invaluable tools in my daily life. There are still challenging days, but I no longer feel at the mercy of my anxiety.

This journey has taught me that healing is not linear. It is a daily commitment to myself, filled with small victories and occasional setbacks. But with each passing day, I grow stronger, more resilient, and better equipped to face whatever challenges lie ahead – not just for myself, but for my family as well.

***The real voyage of discovery consists not in seeking new landscapes, but in having new eyes.* - Marcel Proust**

The Transformative Power of Positive Psychology

In my quest to better understand and support my family, I discovered positive psychology—a revelation that profoundly altered our approach to mental well-being. Unlike traditional psychology's focus on treating mental illness, positive psychology emphasises prevention and the cultivation of psychological strengths. It offers tools for individuals without diagnosed mental health issues to maintain and enhance their overall well-being.

As I delved deeper into this field, I recognised its potential to complement the professional treatment my children were receiving. Positive psychology presented strategies for building resilience, practising gratitude, and finding meaning—skills that could benefit everyone in our family, regardless of their current mental health status.

My daughter's journey particularly illuminated the power of this approach. As she recovered from anxiety and depression with professional help, she chose to volunteer with elderly people. This decision beautifully aligned with the PERMA model of well-being: Positive emotions, Engagement, Relationships, Meaning, and Accomplishment. While volunteering did not directly treat her condition, it seemed to bolster her recovery and enhance her overall sense of well-being.

Inspired by these insights and eager to help other parents facing similar challenges, I decided to pursue a Graduate Diploma in Applied Positive Psychology. My goal was two-fold: to equip myself with tools to maintain our family's mental health and to potentially help others prevent mental health issues.

The course was transformative. I learned evidence-based techniques to enhance well-being, including methods for cultivating gratitude, practising mindfulness, and building resilience—all crucial skills for maintaining good mental health. The concept of flourishing, which focuses on helping people thrive rather than merely avoiding illness, particularly resonated with me.

As we began incorporating these principles into our daily lives, I observed a gradual yet significant shift in our family dynamics. We started celebrating small victories more frequently, practising gratitude regularly, and approaching challenges with a growth mindset. While these practices did not replace professional treatment for my children, they fostered a more supportive environment for their ongoing recovery.

It is crucial to emphasise that positive psychology is not a cure for mental illness and should not substitute professional mental health treatment. However, I have found it to be an invaluable complement to our family's overall approach to mental health, helping us build a foundation of well-being and resilience.

This journey has not only provided us with practical tools for maintaining mental health but has also rekindled our sense of hope and purpose. It highlights the importance of taking proactive steps in mental health care and reveals the potential for growth and positive change even in the face of significant challenges.

As I reflect on our experiences, I feel a strong calling to share this knowledge with other parents and caregivers. I have witnessed firsthand how positive psychology can support and enhance the recovery process, not just for those directly affected by mental health issues, but for entire families. By sharing these insights and techniques, I hope to empower other parents to create nurturing environments that promote mental well-being and resilience in their families.

In the end, this journey through positive psychology has shown me that while we cannot always control the challenges life presents, we can cultivate the strengths and skills to face them with greater resilience and hope. It is this message of empowerment and possibility that I am passionate about sharing with other parents navigating the complex landscape of mental health within their family.

The greatest discovery of my generation is that human beings can alter their lives by altering their attitudes of mind. **- William James**

A Mission to Empower and Support Others

My journey into positive psychology led me to pursue a Graduate Diploma in Coaching, pushing me beyond my comfort zone, particularly in confronting my fear of being observed and public speaking. This experience not only complemented my knowledge but also equipped me with practical tools to support others in their well-being journeys.

I want to take a moment to express my deepest gratitude to my son. His journey has been incredibly challenging, yet he continues to persevere. There was a time when he could not see himself living past 21, and now, even though he is just trying to get by, that shift represents a profound sense of hope. He may not see it himself, but every day he continues to try is a victory. His resilience in the face of such adversity is truly inspiring. It reminds us that progress, no matter how small it may seem, is still progress. His journey emphasises the importance of patience, understanding, and never giving up hope, even in the darkest times.

As I began sharing our family's story through blog posts, I made a startling discovery: mental health challenges were far more prevalent than I had realised, touching almost every family I knew. This revelation shifted my perspective on the stigma surrounding mental health and reinforced my belief in the power of open dialogue and community support.

My first public talk on "Building Resilience and Wellness in Families" at a local community workshop was a humble but profound experience. Though attendance was small, the diverse challenges faced by the parents who came reaffirmed the importance of fostering gratitude and resilience in our daily lives. This event ignited a passion in me to create safe spaces for others to overcome their limitations, recognising that by facing my own fears, I could inspire others to do the same.

Now, my mission extends beyond my family. I am dedicated to reaching out to families from various backgrounds, especially those with limited access to mental health resources. **Through educational workshops on mental health awareness and prevention, I share tools from positive psychology to help build resilience and maintain well-being.** I have found that many parents from various backgrounds often struggle silently with their children's mental health challenges. By sharing our experiences and lessons learned, I hope to provide hope and practical guidance for these families.

In addition to workshops, I offer one-on-one coaching sessions to help individuals develop personalised strategies for maintaining mental wellness and navigating life's challenges. While I always emphasise that I am not a substitute for professional mental health treatment, I can offer support in implementing positive psychology practices in daily life.

As I continue this work, I am driven by the belief that everyone deserves to feel understood, valued, and supported in their journey towards well-being. Each conversation we have brings us closer to a world where mental health is prioritised and where recovery and growth are seen as possible for all.

We rise by lifting others. - **Robert Ingersoll**

Recognising Struggles and Finding Support - A Holistic Approach

Through our family's journey with mental health challenges, I have learned the critical importance of recognising when someone is struggling. Early recognition can make a significant difference in the path to recovery.

Key signs to watch for include changes in sleep patterns or appetite, withdrawal from social activities, difficulty concentrating, persistent negative emotions, loss of interest in activities, unexplained physical symptoms, and mood swings.

If you notice these signs, it is crucial to seek help. Here are some practical steps for getting the best care:

- Consult a mental health professional: A psychologist or psychiatrist can provide a proper diagnosis and treatment plan.
- Be open with your primary care physician: They can rule out physical causes and provide referrals to specialists.
- Explore support groups: Sharing experiences with others facing similar challenges can be incredibly beneficial.
- Consider holistic approaches: Explore complementary therapies like nutrition, exercise, and mindfulness practices.
- Educate yourself: Learn about the specific mental health challenges you or your loved one are facing.
- Create a supportive environment: Make sure home and work environments are as stress-free and supportive as possible.

In addition to professional care, positive psychology exercises can be incredibly powerful in supporting mental health. Here are some practices to try:

- Gratitude Journaling: Write down three things you are grateful for each day.
- Strengths Spotting: Identify and celebrate strengths in yourself and others. Consider taking the VIA Character Strengths Survey **(https://www.viacharacter.org)**
- Acts of Kindness: Perform a small act of kindness daily.
- Mindfulness and Savouring: Practise being present and fully appreciating positive moments.

- Goal Setting: Set small, achievable goals and celebrate your progress.
- Social Connection: Nurture your relationships.
- Positive Reframing: Look at challenging situations from different perspectives to find potential positive aspects.

By combining professional care with holistic approaches and positive psychology practices, we can create a comprehensive strategy for mental health and well-being. This multi-faceted approach builds resilience, fosters positive emotions, and improves overall quality of life.

The greatest discovery of all time is that a person can change his future by merely changing his attitude. **- Oprah Winfrey**

Conclusion: A Light in the Darkness

Looking back on our family's journey, I feel a profound sense of purpose and hope. What began as a personal struggle has evolved into a mission to support others facing similar challenges.

This Mental Health Day, I extend a hand to all who are struggling. Remember, you are not alone. Seeking help is a sign of strength, not weakness. By sharing our stories and supporting each other, we can break the stigma surrounding mental health and foster a more compassionate community.

Our journey has taught us invaluable lessons about resilience, compassion, and the power of family support. We have learned that healing is not linear, but a journey with its own rhythm of progress and setbacks. We have discovered the importance of celebrating small victories and finding joy in quiet moments.

As we move forward, let us continue to speak openly about mental health and work towards creating a world where everyone feels supported in their journey towards well-being. Together, we can build a future where mental health is a priority, where prevention is as crucial as treatment, and where recovery is seen as achievable for all.

Courage doesn't always roar. Sometimes courage is the quiet voice at the end of the day saying, 'I will try again tomorrow. **– Mary Anne Radmacher**

To find out more about me and stay in touch visit:

Linktree: www.linktr.ee/savvyminds

CHAPTER 14

By Samantha Thistlewaite

The Journey of Courage

I shouldn't have known, but maybe I should have guessed, that my hormone journey was never going to be an easy ride. The signs were there early, like the universe nudging me and whispering, "Buckle up, this is going to be a wild one." I was just ten years old, a positive, happy go lucky little girl who had barely begun to understand the world, let alone the chaos of womanhood, when my first period hit me like a ton of bricks. And where did it decide to make its grand debut? The airport, of all places. We had just touched down in Corfu, and while everyone else was excitedly shuffling through arrivals, I was dealing with a very different kind of arrival.

I remember the shock, that sinking feeling of dread mixed with confusion. What was happening to me? Why now? My mum was in full "holiday mode," stressing over the luggage, and there I was, desperately trying to muster up the courage to tell her that my life had just taken a very unexpected turn. The words stuck in my throat, awkward and foreign, as I tried to make sense of this new reality. A week in Corfu should have been a dream, but instead, I spent it feeling self conscious and uncomfortable, trying to navigate life with pads that felt thicker than a brick. This, as it turned out, was just the beginning of a journey that would test every ounce of courage I had.

As if that first experience wasn't enough, my hormone health continued to haunt me through adolescence. Each month was a battle, a week off from school every cycle as I wrestled with debilitating pain and fatigue. Convincing my teachers that my absence was genuine was a struggle in itself. My mum, an incredible woman with love and compassion, fought my corner as she could see her daughter able to do nothing at home except lay in her bed and sleep.

How could I explain that sometimes, the pain was so intense that my legs would literally give out from under me? I remember one particularly mortifying day, collapsing on my way to class because my period was so heavy, my body simply couldn't keep up. My friends at school Jess and Jenny on either side of me helped me walk to the head mistress's office to ask to go home, yet again. Another eye roll, I became used to them as they would follow me through life, if only my internal challenges could've been seen externally, maybe then I'd have had more compassion from others. It was like living in a horror movie where the villain was my own body, and there was no escape.

This plague of period pain followed me relentlessly, refusing to release its grip even after I conceived my first child. Pregnancy, I thought, would be my reprieve. And in some ways, it was, though not without its own set of challenges. I fell pregnant with my first child, a beautiful baby boy, but instead of the blissful, glowing pregnancy that I had imagined, I was plunged into a battle with preeclampsia. My days were spent in and out of the hospital, each visit a reminder that nothing in my life would ever come easily. I would dread my midwife check ups because I knew it would mean a day on a ward or maybe a few being monitored closely, and pricked like a pin cushion with constant blood tests.

Hormones, Hope, and Heartache

Yet, amidst the turmoil, there was joy. I got to be a mum, and despite the rollercoaster of hormones, those early days with my son were some of the happiest of my life. For a time, my hormones seemed to settle, and I dared to hope that the worst was behind me. But life has a funny way of throwing curveballs just when you think you're in the clear. After my second pregnancy, everything came crashing down. I hit 30, and it was as if my body decided to wage an all out war against me.

The bleeding became relentless, often so heavy that I would have to leave work just to go home and change my clothes. It was humiliating, frustrating, and utterly exhausting. I made countless trips to the GP, each time hoping for answers, but all I got were dismissals. Stomach pain? Must be IBS. The pain of living with a condition that no one seemed to understand or believe in was enough to make anyone lose hope. But something inside me refused to give up. I started keeping a diary, meticulously tracking my symptoms, determined to prove that this was not all in my head.

Finally, a locum doctor mentioned the possibility of endometriosis. For the first time, I felt a flicker of relief. I wasn't crazy; there was a name for what I was experiencing. I went home and dove into research, devouring every piece of information I could find. It was like looking in a mirror—every symptom, every struggle, it all made sense. My persistence, my refusal to back down, had finally paid off. But as I would soon learn, this was just the beginning of a much longer battle.

The wait for an MRI felt like an eternity, and when I finally had it, the silence that followed was deafening. No news, no follow-up, just more uncertainty. More trips to the GP, where I practically begged them to look at the MRI results. When they finally did, it was confirmed: moderate endometriosis. Moderate, they called it. As if the pain that had been tearing me apart from the inside could be neatly categorised on a scale. But at least now I had a diagnosis, something to hold onto as I prepared for the next step—a surgery in July 2020.

The surgery revealed the full extent of the damage. My ovary was attached to my bowel, endometriosis had infiltrated my sigmoid colon, and a pelvic clearance was necessary. They say knowledge is power, but in this case, it felt more like a curse. Despite the operation, I was still in excruciating pain, so much so that functioning on a daily basis became nearly impossible. I was running a business, trying to keep it together on the outside, while on the inside, I felt like I was dying. It took every ounce of inner strength and courage I had to keep going, to keep smiling, to keep pretending that everything was okay when it clearly wasn't.

I really felt the gynaecologist dismiss me inside his head, before I'd even began talking. It made me feel like it was all in my head, that I was somehow exaggerating my symptoms. But then they offered me a glimmer of hope: the medical menopause injection. Desperate for relief, I took it in January 2022. And for a while, it was a miracle. The endometriosis pain subsided, and for the first time in years, I could bend, move, and live without agony. But as always, there was a catch. The hot flushes were unbearable, turning even a simple dinner out with my parents into a comedy of errors as I constantly took my coat on and off, caught between the extremes of heat and cold.

I couldn't live like that, and so I made the difficult decision to stop the injections. At my next check-up, I explained to the gynaecologist that while the injections had helped my endometriosis, they had made life otherwise unliveable. Once again, they seemed reluctant to take me seriously, but I trusted my instincts. This confirmed for me what I had suspected all along—my issues were deeply rooted in my hormones. It was time for the ultimate step, one that would require more courage than anything I had faced before: a hysterectomy.

The months leading up to the surgery were some of the darkest of my life. I genuinely believed that I was dying, that the doctors had missed something critical, that I wouldn't survive to see my children grow up. I had never felt so unwell, so utterly broken. For the first time in my life, I gave up. I couldn't work, couldn't fight anymore. And then, just when I thought I had reached my lowest point, I got the call. I could have the hysterectomy. It felt like someone was watching over me, giving me the strength to go on.

The surgery was a success, but the aftermath was a revelation. It turned out that my bladder function was at 20%, and my bladder had been completely repositioned. The endometriosis had been all over my internal pelvis, ovaries, and pouch of Douglas—it was extensive, to say the least. But with the hysterectomy, I began to feel more human again. The physical pain had finally subsided, but a new battle was just beginning: menopause.

When the Body Fails, Courage Prevails

Recovery was a constant struggle, exacerbated by recurring bouts of endometriosis. I was caught in a cruel Catch-22: take HRT and suffer from endo, or avoid HRT and be tormented by menopause symptoms. It was a no-win situation, and my mental health took a severe hit. My weight ballooned, my confidence plummeted, and I found myself withdrawing from the world. Crippling anxiety, overwhelming self-doubt, and relentless hot flushes made everyday life feel like a nightmare. The insomnia was perhaps the worst of it, leaving me feeling like a zombie, unable to function.

The nearly two years post-hysterectomy were some of the hardest of my life, even more so than the physical pain of endometriosis. I had been strong enough to face the physical pain, but the mental toll was a different beast entirely. It's easy for people to say, "Just fix your mindset," but when you're in the throes of such deep despair, those words feel like a slap in the face. It took time—more time than I would have liked—to reach a place where I could see that I was worthy, that I was strong enough to survive this.

Even now, I struggle with my weight, my mindset and so much more, but I remind myself that I'm only human. It's a constant battle, one that ebbs and flows with my mental state. But I've found ways to cope, to take my health into my own hands. Fasting, for example, has been a game-changer for me. It has helped with inflammation, weight loss, and most importantly, with my mental clarity. It's given me a sense of control, something I desperately needed after feeling like my body had been at war with itself for so long.

Through all of this, I've found purpose in helping others who are on similar journeys. I run a Facebook group where I share tips on fasting for menopause health, and I've become a part of the Plymouth Menopause Network. It's a way for me to give back.

Looking back, it's clear that courage has been the thread that ties my entire journey together. From that terrified ten year old girl in Corfu to the woman I am today, every step of the way has required me to dig deep, to find strength I didn't know I had. There were moments when I wanted to give up, when the pain—both physical and mental—felt like too much to bear. But I didn't. I kept going. And in the end, that's what courage is all about. It's not about being fearless; it's about facing your fears head-on, even when every part of you wants to run in the opposite direction. My journey isn't over, and I know there will be more challenges ahead. But I also know that whatever comes, I'll face it with the same courage that has carried me this far.

This is a journey I know that's more than an uphill battle and for support my inbox is always open so add me on Facebook and use my inbox in your times of need when you need a love and kindness.

Contact me at:

Facebook: www.facebook.com/plymouthcleaner

CHAPTER 15

By Lakshmi Dev

Overcoming the Seemingly Impossible

The journey from being a shy and insecure girl to who I am today has been remarkable. I used to be filled with fear and worry about every little thing, turning the most minor concern into a giant, invisible monster. I was a scared little girl. I've since discovered that overcoming childhood traumas and building a life filled with peace that feels purposeful by embracing my unique identity is completely possible.

While I never expected to encounter as many challenges as I have, each has made me stronger and more resilient. I once believed I was inherently flawed, something was wrong with me no matter what I did, and money was only for lucky people. However, I now live with my mind serving my soul.

Despite facing numerous difficult experiences, it's possible to achieve anything by staying true to yourself and drawing upon your inner strength. I am living proof that with determination and self-belief, anything is achievable. As that scared & quiet little girl who couldn't even handle a thunderstorm, I never imagined that I'd now be traveling the world as a transformation catalyst for hundreds of women, sharing my healing gifts from stages as an intuitive DJ in my late 40's, and having over 20 years of certifications under my belt. In other words, you can overcome the seemingly impossible.

Self-Hatred Begins with My Body

Have you ever felt like you didn't fit in? As if everyone else was pretty, popular, and had an easy life? You looked at them and thought, "I wish I were her. She has a real house, nice clothes, all the cabbage patch dolls, and her mom & dad love each other. Why can't I have a normal life?" That is precisely how I felt.

By the time I was ten years old, my parents had already been divorced; I had become a victim of sexual abuse and had moved from a home to switching apartments and schools at least five times, while also being put in unstable situations. I started living a life of comparison that made me believe I wasn't good enough. Those feelings became an inner reflection of how I saw my body. I recall, at nine years old, an incident where I was completely ashamed of my body. My sister had a friend over, and we had to wash up in the sink because the tub wasn't working. I had the door shut and was standing there naked with my head over the sink, rinsing my hair, and she and the friend walked in. I completely freaked out! I remember being so embarrassed, crying, and screaming at them to get out. I felt so much fear and shame around being seen without my clothes on. It's the first of many more memories I have of my body not being acceptable.

At 14 years old, I had already created a story that because there was something wrong with me, there was most definitely something wrong with my appearance. I had been called "Skinny Minny" and told that I ate like a bird, but the one description that was always given to me that made me cringe and want to hide was being told that I had a bubble butt. While it was funny to everyone else and just a part of being a product of my mom's side of the family, it was not okay. This was the year everything changed for me.

As a freshman in high school who was kind of a dork and had the same friends for years, I was ready for something new, and I sure got it. I started drinking and smoking pot with my new friends, which was awesome at the time; "Yes, I finally fit in! Who knew I was this fun and funny?!" I didn't realize it at the time, but the feeling of being drunk and high was my way to escape my inner self-hatred.

This was also the year when my dad, with whom we had a seemingly good relationship but who had been inconsistent in our lives when we were younger due to his struggle with alcoholism, decided that he no longer wanted to see my sister and me. That abandonment wound was reignited, and being a teenager made it harder to deal with. So, I punished myself by becoming anorexic and eventually bulimic. My body was the only thing I felt that I could control.

The downward spiral that began lasted for decades, up until my most significant accomplishment, just over a year ago when I decided to quit alcohol altogether. Believe it or not, I hadn't understood the correlation between my mental struggles and imbalanced emotions being the result of reaching for a drink.

Despite all the studying, practicing, learning, and healing I had dedicated myself to, I still had an inner voice that told me, "This is who I am."

On February 6th of 2020, which happened to be my oldest son's 18th birthday, I was (for the 3rd time in my life) diagnosed with major depressive disorder. This was not new to me, as I had dealt with these feelings throughout my life ever since my first of numerous attempts to escape at 12 years old by ingesting a bunch of Tylenol.

However, this current mental health crisis led to a Divine download that would change everything for me. It took another three years to fully recognize and take responsibility for my life by freeing myself.

The Soul Remedy

If you are dealing with your inner demons that are assholes who hold you hostage, then it's time to put the power back in your hands. We are in a time when the world is run by fear, anger, hatred, and separation. I believe that disconnection at a soul and spiritual level causes panic-driven anxiety, depressive and negative thoughts, worries that feel out of your control, and wanting to curl up and hide from it all. It's not about you having issues. It's about being part of a collective consciousness and generational wounding that takes you away from the true essence of who you are at a soul level. It is not your fault.

The day my Soul Remedy System came about was two days after my MDD diagnosis. I felt I was more of a burden than a necessity, and convinced myself I was a failure as a mom and business owner. I decided to hike and release these energies and my excessively full mind on the Earth. As I ascended the mountain, I told myself, "With every step, I am releasing my pain." When I reached the top of my hike, I felt like a new person. During that process, I cried, I laid on the earth and let her hold me, I placed my hands on her in appreciation of the energy that was being given to me to heal me, and I had a complete shift in my mental and emotional state.

It was then that my big aha came to me. "All that matters is taking time every single day for movement, mother nature, mindset, meditation, and music." This is the remedy my soul needed. As I hiked back out, horses greeted me, a sure sign that what I felt was meant to be. Some symbolism of the horse as medicine is related to overcoming challenges victoriously, healing through spiritual connection, freedom, strength, and courage guiding us like a compass. I realized that I had been giving away my power to old, untrue stories. These were recurring stories about feeling like a burden, not being enough, having something wrong with me, and making wrong choices because I didn't have the right answers.

What's fascinating as I look at how I have served so many others over the last 20-plus years while still moving through pain, is that when you change your perspective, everything in your life will change. This isn't just about a positive mindset, though. This is also, and even more importantly, about the alignment of your energy. Anything or anyone that takes you out of Divine Alignment, including your own subconscious and ego self, will result in some type of self-limitation. Every one of us has our own way(s) that we either limit or sabotage ourselves, one of my biggest being a toxic relationship with alcohol. Yours may be that you procrastinate, use indecisiveness as a form of not taking action, compare to the point of being paralyzed, or maybe you only allow yourself to get so far along and then find a way to negate all that you have accomplished. This is a part of your humanness, yet who you are in the grand scheme of all that exists is a spiritual and soul-light Being in the physical form of a body.

Your Frequency is the Key

The first book that I was ever introduced to around the subject of the mind & body's frequency as a manifestation vessel (that I paid attention to) was "Wishes Fulfilled" (2012) by Dr. Wayne W. Dyer. Before this, I had been in the realm of using meditation and specific spiritual practices through yoga, as well as asking my guides, God, and angels to support me when going through heaviness. I also would do the same when I wanted to create something positive for my future. It seemed as if I could only have so much good happening to me until something went bad. Lucky Me!

Do you struggle with that? You have a vision of your future, but it seems that something is in the way, and you can't quite pinpoint it. In the process of making positive changes, life keeps happening with kids getting sick, spending a mental health day stuck in bed, or flailing while trying to figure out HOW when there is so much to do and not enough of you. It may sound too good to be true, but the only thing that really needs to shift is your frequency. Just like you can't buy a gym membership and expect to get healthy, lose weight, and become stronger without showing up, you also can't have a gorgeous vision for yourself but be committed to a low vibration.

You can read all the books on self-help and manifestation, go to talk therapy, take supplements, practice yoga, and pray your heart out, but if something is off energetically, it won't work. The harsh reality you sometimes don't want to face is that something outside of you will not bring a sense of wholeness within you. Those tools can support you, and I recommend them if they help you to feel better. But you'll continue like the hamster on the wheel until you take full responsibility for eliminating all that's not in full energetic alignment and put the necessary boundaries in place.

You may be thinking, "Well, that's just great! I thought I was on the right track, and now you're telling me I'm wasting my time." That's not what I'm saying. I want you to know that there are ways to make life easier on yourself that may require you to get out of your comfort zone while opening your mind to just how fun it can be.

The hardest thing for us to overcome is our programmed ways of being. I see this in my retreat participants, who want to know every schedule detail before they arrive. They are so accustomed to planning out their daily lives that even considering an open-ended day gives them anxiety because their minds are programmed to ask, "What will I do with myself?" Once they realize that even though there is a tentative schedule, it's much more fulfilling to go with the flow of energy in the group as a whole, they get so much more out of the experience.. Their mind had limited them to do x, at y o'clock, and z will happen. Once their nervous system begins to calm, the desire to be fixated on a set schedule feels forced and the opposite of why they've come in the first place.

And guess what? The golden key to your most yummy frequency is balancing your nervous system. We can get all scientific with this as it's proven that, "Depression leads to changes in autonomic control of the body and changes the autonomic balance in favor of an increased sympathetic tone, which can be detected with fair accuracy with HRV (heart rate variability) analysis," according to the National Institute of Health's National Library of Medicine, 2020. Another aspect that pertains to what I went through is the undeniable link between alcoholism and suicide, as well as alcohol's effect on depression. Its frequency changes you and literally brings you down.

How empowering is that to know?! You control your nervous system, which regulates your mental and emotional state. The more you eliminate negativity from your energetic field, the more stable your nervous system and emotions become.

Putting the Power in Your Own Hands

Through all of my trauma, pain, and sorrow, I have become a version of myself now that I wasn't sure I could ever be. I had a dysregulated nervous system, a dependency on alcohol since my teenage years and a mindset that was pessimistic to protect me from getting my hopes up. I now live oppositely, which has become natural to me. But I had to do it the long and hard way and you don't have to.

Possibly the most exciting piece in all of this is the more fun you have and the less serious you take life, the easier it is to enjoy each day and be in gratitude. Just like a child, you're meant to play, explore, be silly, use your imagination, make new friends, be outside, get lost in goofy shows, and not worry about what's next. The more time you spend being present the more power you put into your own hands. Being present isn't running from emotions or towards an external self-soother.

I truly believe that stepping out of your comfort zone allows you to embrace your truest self, the childlike version of you. Your unique frequency holds the power to transform your mindset, guiding you to unlearn old patterns and embrace a fresh narrative. Finding calm within your nervous system is the key to manifesting the life you dream of. It's about confidently letting go of what no longer aligns with your vision. Embracing these changes will empower you to live a more fulfilling and authentic life.

Here is a simple system to put in place daily so you experience all life has to offer:

1) Spend at least 25 minutes in a combination of some form of Mother Nature, movement, meditation, music, and mindset. You can easily practice each for 5 minutes or create a full combo of them. It may look like walking outside, listening to music, repeating affirmations, and then sitting in silence to soak in gratitude. Your nervous system comes into balance when these are practiced regularly.
2) Make play or pleasure pauses a part of your day. Use your imagination on this one but you can paint, play in the mud, masturbate (yes, that's a powerful form of pleasure), jump & shout, spend time with animals, shake your ass, pretend you're a mermaid, sing as loud as possible, or whatever makes you forget who you are and brings absolute joy. You are energy and letting the mind pause while you get lost in fun elevates your frequency.
3) Commit to your non-negotiables by focusing on who you want to be and what you're creating and take action on those. This is where boundaries come in to no longer allow things, people, or old ways to rule your life. You have the self-will and are more capable than you probably give yourself credit.

If you feel you need help with these, I'm here to support and guide you. After spending years healing, learning, and growing, I know that you can truly overcome the seemingly impossible. You can join one of my international retreats for women, begin an alcohol-free journey with me, or work with me in a group or 1:1 setting to help you uncover your highest potential and live a more purposeful and peaceful life. Find me on Instagram or Facebook @divinelakshmidev and get free access to my Rock Your Chakras video course to follow through on what you believe is best for you if doubt and distraction have held you back. **www.divinelakshmidev.com/r-y-c**

Life is Meant to be Lived and Loved

I understand that for those who have had a painful past, making big changes is not necessarily easy, but you are given the gifts of self-will, inner power, and co-creative capability. Every small step forward adds up to big accomplishments. Each day, remind yourself that you are here to live by being you, overcoming your karma, and being supported by your spiritual self. You have everything you need within. The past is not who you are, although it has defining moments that have strengthened you.

What may seem impossible to overcome now can eventually be a distant memory. I convinced myself that drinking while being all spiritual was "balance." Anyone who knew me before knew me as a fun and crazy party girl but didn't realize my inner struggle. I am still a fun and crazy person who loves to have a good time. It doesn't result in regret, memory loss, or worrying about my health now. I honor myself for who I was and who I've become. I needed all of her. Living with integrity and without the constant battle of my demons running the show is true freedom.

I wouldn't feel complete if I didn't share that I have a wonderful support system of my husband and three kids. While I made major changes in my life for them, I did it for me first. You have to put yourself before anyone else, or it won't work. You deserve to have a life you love.

*www.ncbi.nlm.nih.gov/pmc/articles/PMC7530411/

CHAPTER 16

By Laurie Butson

"One day you will tell your story of how you overcame what you went through, and it will be someone else's survival guide." – Brene Brown

I saw this quote early in my autoimmune disease diagnosis, and it didn't have particular relevance to me. At first. However, as the months went on, this quote became a pillar in my healing. It helped me to begin to uncover my purpose, as it helped me see the journey I was on in a different light. So often we ask ourselves: why is this happening to me? And this quote helped me turn that question on its head and instead ask myself: what can I learn from this?

It would soon become not only a helpful reasoning and analysis tool as I explored the past, but also a grounding and mindfulness mechanism in the present, and a powerful motivator, as I looked to the future.

Can You Flourish with a Chronic Illness?

Whether someone could flourish with a chronic illness is not a question I had ever considered and certainly not one I ever thought I would be asking and answering for myself.

But there I was in February 2023 asking myself this exact question: can I flourish with a chronic illness? And, at the time, honestly, I was unsure of my answer.

Today, as I share my story, I am a firm and committed believer that YES, you absolutely can flourish with a chronic illness or condition. That is why I am so passionate about telling my story and sharing this purpose with the world.

However, like many others, I wasn't immediately able to answer it enthusiastically, but I can now, and I believe others can too.

You see, I am a huge believer that things happen the way they are meant to happen. The years leading up to 2023 had all unfolded exactly the way they were meant to unfold.

My Journey into Positive Psychology

At the start of the pandemic in 2020, I immediately felt that we had an opportunity to focus on mental health in a way that hadn't emerged before. Suddenly we were all going through a collective experience where we were not OK, together. Those who never considered their mental health and overall well being realized that they were not OK. And guess what? That was OK.

I decided early on that I wanted to be part of keeping the focus on and conversation going around mental health and overall wellbeing. I could see we were starting to talk about it in a different way. More people, as well as workplaces, were becoming part of that conversation and bringing it to the forefront. I wanted to do my part in ensuring that continued.

I posted on a local Mom's Group on Facebook that I was looking for something I could do or learn to help others focus on mental health. At the time, I didn't really know what I was asking for or what I wanted to do. I just knew I needed to do something. I knew I wanted to help.

Another mom suggested exploring Positive Psychology. I had never heard of it, but quickly became immersed in learning about it. Discovering it was the science of wellbeing and human flourishing sounded perfect. I immediately knew this is what I needed in my life.

I started out completing a nine-month certification program to become a positive psychology practitioner. I took a deep dive into the science and evidence-based practices behind the science. Over the next few years, I completed almost every certification program offered by The Flourishing Center, based in New York City. I became certified as a practitioner, consultant, resilience trainer, and coach. The more I learned, the more I wanted to learn.

I was genuinely excited to bring all this new knowledge to my organization. I became a spokesperson and the face of mental health and overall wellbeing. I was leading training workshops, doing interviews with internal and external executives, coaching colleagues, advocating for wellbeing initiatives, building wellbeing programming, and more.

Little did I know my own health was deteriorating drastically at the time. I knew my work was stressful, but I didn't realize the toll it was taking on me in many ways, day after day.

My Diagnosis

In the fall of 2022, I slowly started to notice signs of sickness. My body didn't feel right, but I couldn't put my finger on what was going on. My joints hurt and my body ached. At first, I was convinced it was Lyme disease. I have a black lab, who I adore, and living in the mountains, we are out hiking every day. Like many of us so often do, I ignored my symptoms for as long as I could, and I put up with the annoyance. Because that was what it was at first, an annoyance.

Over the weeks to come, it became much more than annoyance and I needed to go to the doctor. Like many with chronic illness, it took quite a while, multiple appointments, and several doctors until I finally got my diagnosis.

I had self-diagnosed in the months of the unknown and so it wasn't overly surprising that during my first visit to a rheumatologist that I was diagnosed with the autoimmune disease, Rheumatoid Arthritis. There are many things I remember from that first appointment, but the one that has played repeatedly in the months since was my doctor saying: your body didn't get this sick overnight, and it's not going to heal overnight either.

It wasn't until months later that I truly understood the magnitude of that statement. I hadn't had an illness before that wasn't cured in a short time frame. I certainly didn't have anything that I would have for the rest of my life.

Before getting sick, I barely knew what an autoimmune disease was, and I definitely didn't know what Rheumatoid Arthritis was. I told my doctor at the time that I had started eating an anti-inflammatory diet, secretly hoping that would be "enough" and I could continue that path as I started my healing. My doctor commended me on the dietary changes and encouraged me to keep that up, but also explained that my body was very sick and at risk of getting much worse, much more quickly, without medication.

As I left that first appointment, I knew I had a lot to learn. I was ok with going the medication route, as I trusted what my doctor explained about both the disease and the severity of it that I currently had. That said, I also vowed as I drove home from that appointment that I was going to tackle my diagnosis, and subsequent recovery, with everything I had and look at it as holistically as possible, beyond medication.

The Early Days of Diagnosis

I always considered myself a relatively healthy person. I played sports growing up and in college. I ran a half marathon a few years before getting sick. Exercise was a regular part of my life. I also felt I was relatively mentally healthy. Heck, I was the voice and the face of mental health for my organization. How could I not be mentally healthy?

However, I also quickly learned that there is so much I didn't know about physical and mental health. While I was doing a lot right, I also had a lot of room for improvement and growth.

I tried to juggle and live a normal life for the first several months. I had handled big things before, so for sure I could continue to do it all. I had a complex, stressful job that I tried to maintain both my pace and my success at. I was a wife and the mom of teenagers, with a fabulous and busy family that I tried to keep up with. But I also now had a new diagnosis and was in significant pain every day. After a few months, I realized I wasn't being successful at anything. I wasn't getting better. I felt like I was failing at every aspect of life. Most importantly my health was not improving.

In consultation with my doctor, I decided to take a medical leave from work to focus on getting myself healthier. At first, I decided to take six weeks off and told everyone I thought I'd be back early. Six weeks felt like an eternity. But those six weeks quickly turned into 13 weeks, as it was abundantly clear that what my doctor told me in that first appointment was accurate – I wasn't going to heal overnight.

Taking a medical leave will remain one of the best things I have ever done for myself. I committed to myself that my "job" during that leave was to wake up every day and ask myself what does my body need today to heal?

The first couple of weeks were OK. Without the stress and with the responsibility of my job gone, I thought I felt a little better. Until I didn't. About three weeks into my leave, my body got worse. Much worse. I went through a three-week period of not being able to move my body every morning upon waking. It was as though my body froze in place overnight.

Slowly I would start to move each part of my body to wake it up and "thaw" each part out. Throughout the day I was able to 'improve'. By the end of the day, I always felt a little better. But my barometer was low. When each morning I couldn't move, feeling a little better didn't take much and my life and body didn't look anywhere close to normal.

Looking back on that three-week period, I am now able to say that I am grateful a significant flare happened. It was, again, a reminder of how sick my body was and how much attention it needed. It catapulted me into a new realm of healing.

Could I Flourish with a Chronic Illness?

I was able to admit that my current medication wasn't working. I found my way into one of the best hospitals in the country. I knew this doctor would be a relationship and partnership that I'd have for the rest of my life, and I wanted to be in the best care.

I also knew I had to double down on my mental health and overall wellbeing. In that three-week period, I could feel myself slipping into a dark place. I was sad, angry, scared, and most of all not feeling hopeful.

This is about the time in my health journey when I started to ask myself the question of whether you can flourish with a chronic illness. I wholeheartedly wanted to answer yes, but in those early days, I wasn't sure.

Never in a million years could I have imagined that I would have the opportunity to put all that I had been studying, learning, and teaching about Positive Psychology over the prior four years to practice – on myself. I set out to answer the question about whether I could flourish with a chronic illness.

Creating My Own Illness-Wellness Continuum

During my Positive Psychology studies, I had learned about the Two Contina Model of Mental Health by Dr. Corey Keyes. Simply put, this model showed that just because you don't have a mental illness, it doesn't mean that you are mentally well. And in reverse, if you have a mental illness that doesn't mean you can't still flourish, with the right awareness, support, resources, and tools to focus on your mental health and wellbeing. This was one of my favorite models and concepts to talk about because it dispelled so many myths. I think there are huge misconceptions in our society in both directions. That if you don't have a diagnosis, that you must be mentally well and that if you do have a diagnosis of a mental illness, that you can't still thrive. Both of those couldn't be further from the truth.

I started to think more about this model and started to envision a revised version of it focused on chronic physical illness, versus mental illness. I decided this would be the premise of my experimentation of whether I could still thrive and flourish with a chronic illness. If what I believed to be true and you could flourish with a mental illness, I was ready to put to the test replacing a mental illness with a physical illness to see if one could still flourish. It was at that moment that I knew I had a gold mine at my disposal. I had all the tools I needed to see if I could thrive with a chronic illness. I had the science of Positive Psychology.

In the weeks and months to come, I started to apply my learnings, teachings, and expertise to myself. I focused not only on healing my body physically, but also ensuring I was equally focused on my mental health and overall wellbeing. I became my own student and my own case study.

Overview of Positive Psychology

The science of Positive Psychology is vast. There have been decades of research and evidence-based studies developed. Given my background of being a practitioner, consultant, and coach, I had many tools to draw upon as I focused on my wellbeing. A key premise of Positive Psychology is to focus on what's right vs. what's wrong and to build more of that.

One of the things I appreciate most about the science of positive psychology is that it recognizes that flourishing is made of many components and it's different for each of us. There are six pathways to human flourishing, and I will share some examples of the ways I tapped into the science to pave my own path to flourishing.

Positive Emotions

I am a firm believer that all emotions are beneficial. When I teach and coach others, I am the first to say that we want to feel, experience, and understand what our emotions are trying to tell us. I am particularly a believer in the importance of understanding what the negative emotions are trying to tell and teach us, by listening to them and working through them. I had many negative emotions in the early days of my journey. These ranged from sadness, grief, confusion, uncertainty, and more. Rather than ignore them or suppress them (which we too often do), I truly felt them and learned from them. It was through many of my negative emotions that I was able to realize what was important to me and become even more motivated to make changes.

On the other hand, we can induce positive emotions. Many times, the positivity simply wasn't there, but that didn't mean that good wasn't there. I believe even in our darkest moments, there is always good, something to learn, and things to be grateful for. One tool that was incredibly meaningful to me was Three Good Things, where I identified three good things that happened each day and I was grateful for. The days when it was harder to find them were the days I needed to do the exercise the most.

Engagement

I tapped into using my strengths during my healing. One of my top strengths is love of learning. I threw myself fully into learning about autoimmune disease and rheumatoid arthritis. I didn't want to be a bystander in my life and in my health journey. I wanted to be leading my own way. I learned the role that stress plays. I learned the role of our nervous system and how dysregulated it can be (from stress and other things) and the power of paying attention to our nervous system and reregulating it.

My top character strength is Honesty. I directed it towards myself and became crystal clear – I knew I needed to make changes in my life, and I was honest with myself about what those changes were. Some were big and some were small. Some were easy and some were incredibly difficult. One of the most significant areas I focused on was stress. Stress is a terrible trigger for autoimmune conditions and because of this, I made the decision to leave my 25-year corporate career to start my own business. Was it scary? Absolutely. Was it worth it? To this day, I will tell anyone that it's one of the best decisions I made in my healing journey.

Relationships

Some days it was easy to hide and to want to shut the world out. I felt as though no one understood what I was going through. Fortunately, I have an amazing husband who was all in with me. He said from the beginning that this was "our" journey we were on together, not just mine. He always made me feel like we were partners in figuring it out together. My children were also instrumental in my healing. They were curious, helpful, supportive, and strong. I am the first to realize how blessed I am in that regard. I know many partners and families do not support those living with chronic illness. But there are people out there that you can tap into and it's important to find them. For some that might be in the immediate family. For others it might be friends or community members.

I also developed what I called "Laurie's Care Team." As I slowly started to get to know my body all over again, and what it needed from me, I sought out many people to help me with care for my body. On my care team I had people who did massage, yoga, a nutritionist, friends, family, and many others.

Meaning

I was fortunate to find meaning in my diagnosis and subsequent recovery. This was perhaps the most surprising area for me and brings me back to my opening quote: "One day you will tell your story of how you overcame what you went through, and it will be someone else's survival guide."

I had been wanting to start my own business for quite some time, but it was scary leaving a secure job that I liked. But I also quickly realized that one of the reasons I was going through what I was going through was to be able to use my journey and my gifts to help others.

Achievement

Most days it was a blessing to get through the day. But I also understood the significance of setting goals, no matter how small they might be and working towards those goals. At first those goals looked like learning how to move my body again. In the many months I didn't know what was wrong with my body, I didn't move it. I was too scared. I didn't know why I was in so much pain and I didn't want to make it worse, so my body became stagnant out of pain and fear. I started out with small goals like walking to the end of the driveway and back. I knew the importance of setting achievable and realistic goals to help me feel like I could have authority over making them happen. Over time, I was able to make different and bigger goals.

Another key area in my healing journey was coaching. One of the huge benefits of being a coach is being surrounded by other fantastic coaches. I opened myself to coaching and was coached several times a week. Each session I would show up to it vulnerably and ready to work on whatever I was facing that day. The beauty in a coaching partnership is the focus on the future and what you are trying to achieve. These coaching partnerships kept me focused, accountable, and motivated.

Vitality

I was far from living a life of vitality in my early days of diagnosis. I realized I needed to get to know my body all over again and determine what it needed from me to heal. This included movement, sleep, nutrition, body work, and learning about many different healing modalities. I knew my body needed many different things from me. One of the biggest shifts I made was around realizing my body and I were a team. At first, I was angry at my body for "doing this to me" but over time, I realized that it wasn't my body against me. We were in this together. Mind, body, spirit, and soul.

As I look back on these six areas, I can't say that one was more important than another. Rather, every part was its own unique piece of my healing puzzle. I am a firm believer that there's not one thing that makes us unwell, and therefore, there's not just one thing that will make us well.

Building your own puzzle and fitting together the right pieces is unique to each of us.

I CAN Flourish with a Chronic Illness

As I write this, I am about to approach the two-year mark of when my symptoms first started. It's incredible to look back over the past two years and look at everything I've been through. I am not the same person that I was two years ago. While I wouldn't wish the pain of Rheumatoid Arthritis on anyone, I also wouldn't change anything that I've been through, as I believe I am exactly where I am meant to be. I am better off because of RA and all that it has taught me. I am stronger physically, mentally, and emotionally and am in better mental and physical shape than I have been in years. Perhaps my entire life. Now, I am more than ready to continue my passion and purpose to show others that they, too, can flourish with a chronic illness. I now embody this quote wholeheartedly: "One day you will tell your story of how you overcame what you went through, and it will be someone else's survival guide."

How You, Too, Can Flourish with a Chronic Illness

The science of Positive Psychology is deep and vast. If you are ready to build a foundation to flourish, I encourage you to start by answering these simple questions related to each of the pathways.

1) Positive Emotions: what brings you joy and happiness?
2) Engagement: what are your strengths?
3) Relationships: who are the people that bring you the most support?

4) Meaning: what larger purpose do you feel connected to?
5) Achievement: what small goals can you set for yourself?
6) Vitality: what are you doing to take care of your mind, body, and spirit?

In addition, please scan the QR code below to download my free "Flourishing with Chronic Illness Starter Kit" to learn more and to take additional steps to building your foundation of flourishing.

How to Reach Me

I work with workplaces, individuals, and groups, empowering each person I connect with to become more aware of what a flourishing future can look like. I'd be honored to connect with anyone who would like to learn more about Positive Psychology, anyone managing chronic illness and looking to take steps towards flourishing, or those curious to learn more about my journey. You can connect with me by scanning the QR code below.

Thanks, so sincerely, for reading my story.

COURAGE

“ONLY THOSE WHO WILL RISK GOING TOO FAR CAN POSSIBLY FIND OUT HOW FAR ONE CAN GO.”

- T. S. ELIOT

CHAPTER 17

By Shobana Narasimhan

Positive Psychology Coach, Software Industry Professional

Introduction

When I was five, I exchanged the safe haven of my home for the neighborhood kindergarten. On my first day, I was so distressed upon entering the noisy classroom that the bemused teachers ushered me into the staff room, where I sat quietly coloring and poring over picture books. It took close to a week, but eventually, clinging to the teacher's hand, I ventured inside. My anxiety subsided as I joined a group of children sitting on the floor, content to be on the periphery and watching them play.

Today, decades later, a good book and a quiet corner are still my sanctuary. I am still the most comfortable at the periphery of a group, observing from the outside. I am a married mother of two and a first-generation Indian immigrant to the USA, having come for undergraduate studies. I spent over thirty years in the software industry before stepping back at the end of 2023 to pursue my aspiration of building a coaching practice. My story is about navigating the corporate world as a painfully shy introvert, a world that, for much of my career, was built around the extrovert ideal. It's about leaning into my strengths to carve out my identity as a leader while staying true to myself. And it's about my ardent belief that when pressured to change who we are, we must question whether the problem lies with us or with the systems around us.

Finding My Way

My first job, at a software company in Massachusetts, involved testing software for defects before customer release. As a new graduate, I felt out of place amongst my older, mostly male coworkers. But they were friendly and supportive, and eased my entry into the workforce. I loved diving deep into my projects, taking the real-world learnings to heart. When my manager left to join a startup, she hired me into her new team. We got acquired by a California based company, I accepted the offer to relocate, and my Silicon Valley career was launched.

Silicon Valley in the late 1990s was in the midst of the dot com era; a place where exuberance co-existed with a vast hubris fueled by the promise of quick riches and the rise of the celebrity CEO. I sat out the dot com boom, needing to stay with the same employer as I acquired permanent residency. My own life transformed as I got married, and gave birth to a beautiful daughter who faced major health challenges her first year. After a year's leave to care for her, I returned to the workforce in a high-pressure program management role at a large tech company in the Valley. I had exciting projects to work on, a welcoming team, and a supportive manager. But I also faced a demanding pace (all the more challenging as a new mom), and a harsher culture than I was used to. I had entered a school of both rich learning and hard knocks.

Imprinted in my memory are the executive reviews, forums where project and engineering managers would present the status of their projects to leadership. The reviews were notorious for mortifying public rebukes and unpredictable questions that could zone in on a single small mistake. I dreaded those presentations with a vengeance, transported back to childhood fears of getting yelled at by the principal. However diligently I prepared, nervousness could cause me to back myself into a corner and need to be bailed out by more seasoned team members.

I sought advice from colleagues that seemed unperturbed by these interactions. The gist was that I needed to grow a thicker skin and be savvier about spinning my status. I consulted with HR once, and was told that each executive had their own style. At the time, I accepted all of this; later, I was dismayed that we had ever normalized fear and public shaming. We were an incredibly hard-working team, stretching both ends of the day to accommodate an always-on work environment. I would often nurse my son (born 2 years after my daughter) to sleep and then hop right back on my laptop to work –wanting nothing more than to curl up under my duvet but committed to meeting my deadlines. I didn't need to toughen up and learn to improvise a smooth story - it was our execs that needed to feel accountable to create a culture of psychological safety.

If exec reviews were a minefield, regular meetings were their more benign cousins. Large meetings were the platform of choice for sharing ideas, voicing opinions, and making decisions. The problem is that large meetings were also spectacularly incompatible with my personality. For one I was quickly overwhelmed with the cacophony of opinionated people all talking at the same time. Trying to get a word in edgewise was akin to being at a four-way stop–hesitate for a fraction of a second, and you lose your turn. My introvert need to have every sentence be surgically precise and well thought out didn't help. Unsurprisingly, I rarely spoke in meetings and risked coming across as passive or disengaged to those who didn't know me well.

When I did speak up, I wouldn't always get heard. I am soft-spoken, and I got talked over quite a lot. (I don't usually follow internet memes, but I did feel a rueful solidarity with the creator of the #AmIOnMute pandemic-era meme) And sometimes someone else, with less expertise than me, would authoritatively say the same thing and the idea *(my idea)* would get traction.

I mined a few life hacks from the internet. I made sure I said something, anything, during the first few minutes of a meeting. I asked questions, a low-pressure way to participate in a discussion. I essentially worked around a system that wasn't designed for me or for a large percentage of individuals in the workforce.

I was also struggling to balance my naturally collaborative, pragmatic program management approach with more traditional expectations of enforcing rules and wielding the whip. The pernicious "too nice" label emerged and would be my bugbear for years to come. Over time I would comfortably inhabit my style, learning to balance it with directiveness when needed, while accepting that I could not please everyone. But at that time, I questioned my instincts. I was still finding my way.

Finding My Voice

Even as I navigated my obstacles, my professional life was flourishing in other ways. There was abundant camaraderie, lots of laughs, managers who believed in me, and colleagues who lifted me up when I was running on empty. I was learning and growing quickly, garnering respect and expanding my responsibilities. And crucially, I was cementing a strong, positive professional identity that was grounded in my strengths.

I was good at cutting through complexity, structuring realistic plans, and guiding the team to follow those plans. I was good at creating harmony, building relationships, and balancing different perspectives. I could stay steady and tactful under pressure. I was organized and could hone in on what mattered most. I was not the bold visionary–and that was ok. A vision without execution stays a concept, and my role was critical to the business.

As I found my footing, I started to control my own narrative. For instance, I was much stronger at expressing my opinions in writing than at impromptu verbal sparring. Writing would let me reason out my arguments using data (my superpower!) I started sharing my thoughts over email whenever possible, and arranged smaller meetings, where I was much more outspoken. This helped to counteract the "babble effect" where the most talkative people in the group are seen as leaders. By adapting the system, I was finding my voice.

Claiming My Space

A career highlight came when I moved to a group working on a pioneering cloud-hosted product (the cloud refers to software and services that run on the internet, instead of on your computer). We were one of the first cloud-hosted solutions in the company and needed to juggle ambiguous and conflicting requirements across many teams. Tempers were flared, setbacks frequent. It was project management manna, and a chance to prove myself in uncharted territory, and in the end, my hard work to tame the complexity and to create processes where none existed proved critical to a successful launch.

The project was my breakout role, where I transitioned to being seen as a leader. My manager and the group executive, self-described introverts, intuitively understood and provided what I needed–a safe, supported seat at the table where I could freely express myself. Feeling seen, heard and appreciated unlocked my mojo.

With increased self-assurance, "nice" and "soft", the four-letter words that were always thrumming in the background, became simply a part of who I (mostly) was and not flaws to fix. I would also argue here that we need to take a far more nuanced view of what "nice" means. Niceness can be ruinous when it hinders boundary-setting or self-expression. But at its heart, niceness embodies empathy, reason, respect, kindness and humility–qualities that elevate the whole team. Nice is good for business!

All that said, I sometimes needed to summon what an early manager and mentor called "a bit of arrogance". She told me that all I needed occasionally was a bit of arrogance, advice that has stayed with me to this day. The closest I can come to describing how this feels for me is to channel (stay with me here) Elsa in Frozen, belting out 'Let It Go'. It was about claiming my space in the world, and releasing, without inhibitions, the power inside. That meant that I'd sometimes rub people the wrong way when I argued my case, and sometimes my decisions would make people unhappy. It meant that when I prevailed in a debate, I needed to own the victory and not feel unnerved and uncomfortable. There was no magic wand to make peace with the dissonance that came with causing ripples, but it was key to have faith that I'd been fair and thoughtful, values that were important to me.

If I could give my younger self some practical advice, it would be to understand early the difference between being assertive and aggressive.

This sentence from the book 'Changing for Good' by James O'Prochaska sums it up beautifully:

"If non-assertive, passive behavior says that 'you count but I don't', and aggressive behavior says that 'I count and you don't', assertiveness respectfully communicates that **'I count just as you do.' "**

The book outlines certain fundamental rights–like the right to be heard, the right to make mistakes, the right to judge our own thoughts and resist the judgment of others. If we are expressing our rights while respecting the other person's, we are communicating assertively. Over the years, there have been many times when I have been passive until my frustration boiled over, or when I have crossed the line into aggression. All of this is human.

There is one meeting that stays with me as a defining moment in claiming my space. I spent twenty five minutes at that meeting challenging a colleague whom I felt had undermined my decision. We each passionately argued our case, and I held my ground, resisting the temptation to concede. My teammates on the call were momentarily stunned into silence witnessing the equivalent of the mild-mannered scientist morphing into the hulk. I wasn't proud that we had wasted other people's time. But I was proud of the healthy personal growth that allowed me to deal with conflict head-on (though I suspect that my colleague - a brilliant engineer - didn't quite see it that way). It sounds so insignificant when I write it down, but that was my Everest.

As my career evolved, I took on team management responsibility. I had managed people earlier in my career, and always enjoyed working with team members one-on-one. But at this stage, working with larger and more distributed teams, I faced higher expectations to establish a visible presence. I once avoided conducting an all-hands meeting for months after I started with a team, convinced that my every word would be judged and found wanting. In a timely spot of reverse mentoring, a young college alum told me that she couldn't remember a word of what her team lead had said at his all-hands–just that it happened, and that was the important thing. I stopped overthinking, enlisted people's help for the content, and all went well.

It was yet another lesson in talking down my inner critic, the voice that demanded perfection, magnified my flaws, and dismissed what I'd accomplished. In micro doses, it was useful for spurring high-quality work and keeping me honest. But mostly, it got in the way. Receiving feedback in particular was exhausting–feedback implied that I had, gasp, made a mistake - and mistakes at work were just not a thing in my critic's universe.

There was again, no magic wand to conquer this. Harnessing empathy to understand the feedback was always helpful. When an executive dismissed a report I had labored over as "a data dump", I threw a quiet tantrum, then went to work trying to fix it. A peer pointed out that the executive simply didn't have the time to decipher pages of numbers and dates. Shifting perspectives to what he needed let me detach from the criticism and focus on making my reports useful to him (and he would later be a strong supporter). I was also increasingly the one giving feedback and asking questions. My angle was **always** to improve how we did things, not to judge the people involved. Knowing this helped me to cut myself some slack.

More recently, during a coaching demo, we were asked what we would say to our inner critic. I found that emphatically talking back to it was a powerful way to neutralize the voice. At that moment, it was telling me that nobody would want to read my story. I countered that it might resonate with just one person, and writing it was fulfilling. That thought centered me through the writing of this chapter.

Creating My Future

In 2019, months before the pandemic rattled the world, a chance exchange on LinkedIn led to a job at another large tech employer. Though this marked a fresh chapter in my professional journey, I was already contemplating a future beyond the software industry. As a manager I loved to give people a supportive space, loved to encourage them and see them rise to a potential that they sometimes didn't see in themselves. I wanted to preserve these aspects of the job in my second act, though I didn't yet know what that looked like. I was also increasingly reflecting on the changes that I'd witnessed in the industry, and how I could use my voice to influence what mattered to me.

The team that I was in during the last few years had an extraordinary culture of psychological safety. We had each other's backs, we communicated openly and we debated respectfully.

It was an environment in which most of us could just be ourselves and thrive. A team culture like this is still rare, but I have seen a heartening trend in tech to be genuinely inclusive of different personalities and styles.

But we can do so much better. To paraphrase philanthropist Melinda Gates, we should not be sending our daughters (or sons) into a workplace designed for our dads–a sentiment that is personal to me as my kids grow up. Conversations about inclusivity have entered the mainstream but we still seem to operate within an archaic echo chamber, in and out of the workplace.

For instance, when tennis star Naomi Osaka withdrew from the 2021 French Open citing the impact on her mental health of media interviews, I wondered if there were more inclusive approaches to media interaction– ones that would respect her communication style and let her focus on her formidable tennis, and I similarly wonder now if we can reimagine workplaces to be environments designed to allow employees to focus on doing their best work.

To take just one example, employees are often advised to advocate for their own promotions and raises.

I accept that this is necessary but it feels so flawed to burden already overworked employees with marketing their work just to get their dues. Leadership coach Patty Azzarello, in her bestselling book 'RISE' recounts a time when she did stellar work but got no pay raise. Her boss's explanation was that "nobody knew her". Her lesson to the reader is self-advocacy, but I have to wonder why her boss didn't consider it part of his job to bolster her visibility. We need to hold senior leaders accountable to implement clear, consistent policies, and managers accountable to understand and reward their team members' contributions.

But what could I do about any of this? I have witnessed small steps leading to big changes over time. I could take small steps in my corner of the world. I tried to ensure that work spoke for itself in my team, and that we respected different communication styles. I championed fixing not the volume of the quieter voices, but our listening skills (along with judicious use of the zoom 'raise hand' function to counter #AmIOnMute!). I regret not speaking up earlier in my career, but am grateful for the growth and safe spaces that enabled me to do so later.

In the end, the decision to walk away from the corporate world was a difficult one, although it had been years in the making. My work had been so much more than a paycheck, providing purpose, structure, mental stimulation and treasured friendships. I was proud of the work I had done and enriched by everything I had experienced. Once, resilience meant bouncing back from setbacks intact, like a Japanese daruma doll. Now, I see it as Kintsugi, finding beauty in the cracks.

Though daunting, walking away liberated me to explore a new path. I had experienced first-hand the transformational effects of support and a safety net, from the teachers who let me sit out kindergarten till I was ready, to the managers that encouraged and brought out the best in me at work. I was captivated by the thought that I could focus on positively impacting people's lives. My decision was sealed.

After I left my corporate job, I started volunteering for the community. I coached people through workplace issues on a support line. I mentored first-generation college students on career readiness and helped recently arrived refugees with job assistance.

Inspired by my experiences, I enrolled in a rigorous coach training program grounded in the science of positive psychology–a strengths based approach that I have always lived by. The path of coaching has been tremendously fulfilling. It speaks to a purpose that goes so much beyond the next project or deadline, and I believe that I would have benefited from having a coach at many points in my life.

As I write this, I am eager to partner with you in designing your future. Whether you want to find your voice, nurture a positive habit or reach an audacious goal, I am committed to guiding you forward harnessing your wisdom and perspective. Drawing on my experiences and training, I will walk with you as you explore your challenges and your possibilities.

Thank you for reading my story. Now, I invite you to pick up your metaphorical pen. What will your story be?

If you enjoyed my story, let's get connected:

Linktree: www.linktr.ee/shobananarasimhan

CHAPTER 18

By Sherry White

Introduction

I spent a long time deciding how open and raw to be in sharing my story. For years, I was closed off, pushing people away, and even hurting them—reflecting the pain I felt within myself. It took me a while to realise, I was treating others how I felt I deserved to be treated, and that was very wrong. Where does that stem from?

Our childhoods. Our experiences at home, at school, where we grow up, and how we transition into adults.

Well, I was bullied, I was quiet. I HATED upper school. I hated who I was, because the people around me made me feel that way. I didn't have perfect hair, or big boobs, or the first clue about makeup! I remember going from having best friends at lower school, to them becoming bullies in middle school. Why? No idea. Girls turn on each other so easily. Everyone was trying to fit into circles, that, as adults, we realize really don't matter. But as growing girls, it's all you can see, and it deeply matters to your developing minds and overwhelming hormones.

So, I will write this as raw, as honest, and as open as I can. By doing that I hope that it might impact at least one person to think differently about themselves, about others, or maybe just feel less alone. I will talk about things that I haven't told many people. I would also like to mention one super special person who inspired me to be more open too by putting himself out there. Mr Ed Jervis, you are an absolute inspiration, and I am in constant awe of you. 🤍

So, what's my story?

My story is a testament to the power of resilience and collaboration. As a businesswoman, mother, and someone who has faced significant personal challenges, I've learned that success isn't just about reaching a destination—it's about navigating the journey with grace, determination, and a commitment to lifting others as you climb.

Anxiety was a constant hum in my background for years, but it really intensified after having twins. My daughter had just turned one when, four days later, I gave birth to twins (yes, you read that right!). After three years of struggling to get pregnant, nature certainly made up for lost time!

Trying to coordinate that many feeds on little to no sleep felt like trying to lift heavy weights while milking a cow, or something that bizarre. But you find ways to manage life, don't you? I became super mum, the most efficient person you could ever meet. I had my feeding schedule, and I had made the conscious decision that breast feeding would just not be on the cards for these two. They spent the first 17 days in the neonatal unit at hospital and my one-year-old wasn't allowed in to avoid the spread of germs. Understandable, but that really made it hard to coordinate around them. They were so small. Things had to be clean.

These little babies started their lives with feeding tubes, and the rush from the hospital to get them home made me even more stressed. I didn't feel at all ready! But here they were, and I had to make sure they survived! Me?! So, I became a bit over the top about things, and bang, anxiety was something going on; yet I had no idea. I thought I was just an epic organiser! I didn't realise how challenging anxiety could become, or that I was even struggling with it.

I thought I avoided going out because it was just too much hassle with 3 small children, not because the preparation required to take them out was something of a marathon. To be able to locate a toilet or changing station or find a place to feed them was just too stressful with all 3 at once, needing different things at different times.

I have always been very ambitious too, wanting to do great things, and wanting to make life better for every good person I meet. I've always been driven, pouring my energy into whatever I'm passionate about. Even during maternity leave, I set up a Facebook business. People often ask me, 'How do you do it all?' The truth is, I just do.

While a strong work ethic can lead to promotions, it can also make you vulnerable to being taken advantage of. I started on a journey into HR because of my strong moral beliefs, and the fact that standing up for things meant I had encountered a lot of poor treatment. Illegal treatment I now know, but there will be another book for that. For all your HR war stories too.

I loved my job. At least that's what I told myself. I genuinely believed it too. Until one day someone said to me "well, why do you love it? You always seem stressed, you're constantly working". That really hit me. I had masked anxiety and stress for so long, but I was clearly unravelling.

I had started medicating for anxiety and depression a few years earlier. But I didn't recognise what was going on. I would be at work during the day, responding to messages during school runs, after work, I would go home, make dinner and keep working. I did not switch off. There were quotes to go out, emails to respond to, systems to build and I was responsible for it all.

But when is enough, enough? When do you realise that your family is there, and time is being lost. They are growing and you are not even watching, let alone participating. Something had to change. Except by that point, I was totally lost and overwhelmed. My mental health had seriously declined. I couldn't stop my mind racing, and my body was like lead. I increased my medication and sought support from my GP.

My once-vibrant spirit was muted, replaced by exhaustion. I feel a lot of Managers end up in this state too, trying so hard to manage up, and down. Being the filter and taking the harsh truth, bottling it up so you don't lose great people. Masking all of that, as well as masking yourself is going to take its toll. My husband was worried. He had never seen me like this. I had no idea what to do. I spent several months in a total blur of tears and confusion with support from professionals.

Then came the word. Redundancy.

Well, it made the decision for me, didn't it.

What next?

So, I set up for myself.

Since doing that, I have spent time really learning who I am and who I want to be, without the identity of a "job title" pinning me down, or goals I had when I was 20 that really were not relevant to my life anymore. I seem to have developed many titles since! But what matters is that now, it is my choice, and I am accountable to myself.

If I work in the evening, I'm working for myself. My goals are set by me. Not someone else and their idea of what I should do and when I should do it. Then having to work out how to fit it all in. If it's the summer holidays and my kids want to watch a movie or go for a walk during the day, I can do that. I'll pick up work later.

It isn't easy by any stretch, but I love it. Genuinely.

I have met some amazing people.

No more schmoozing with people trying to win business.

Now it's genuine conversations. Real partnerships. True alignment.

My goal now is to grow businesses through my consultancy by supporting others to achieve their best. This means focusing on people practices, efficiency, and making balanced business decisions that prioritise people, the planet, and profit. I choose when I work. I choose what to charge, and how to invest money for my business.

What have I learned?

Don't bust your backside for anyone other than yourself.

Find good people and don't give up hope that they exist (I can introduce you to plenty!)

Know your weaknesses. Don't fear them.

In employment, my weakness was taking it all on my own shoulders and struggling between people first principles and ambitious business managers. When things got difficult, I thought I might still have a support network. But apparently, I didn't. That hit hard. The power of fear and manipulation is terrifying to witness, and most people simply shut down and become numb to it, just going along with the day. Suddenly you are fighting alone and not even supported by the people you are fighting for.

People may hurt or disappoint you. People that you care about. But you will bounce back, stronger than before. Why? Because life is bigger than a few rotten eggs. Because you must understand that most people grow up either selfish or afraid. Either way, when shit gets tough, they protect themselves first.

Why can't I just conform?

I've been described as many things. Quirky. Eccentric. Unprofessional (that one certainly pissed me off!) It was only because I can be known to randomly dance in the office at times.

I thought I just came from a bit of a quirky family. My mum was always a bit barmy, and my brother had a whole army of imaginary friends as a kid! My nan used to dance around the room and pull silly faces. It was just good fun, wasn't it? As I aged, it became harder to be me. Teenage years demanded that I be whatever people expected, so I became something that I wasn't at all.

Adult life was challenging in many ways too. Standing up for what was right got me fired. Got me made falsely redundant. Had me fail probation. I'll save those stories for another book. All of them were not for the reasons given officially. They were because I spoke up against things that were wrong. Like selling out of date meat, bullying other staff and refusing staff breaks on 12-hour shifts.

As life became more demanding I started to rely on medication, which worked – to an extent. But there were questions. In the HR world I see a lot now about inclusion, and I absolutely advocate for fair treatment – for everyone. So, I started talking to people about Neurodiversity. I didn't think much of it at first, until I started to learn more. I think like a lot of people, I thought it was more than what I was dealing with. There isn't nearly enough education anywhere around what it really means to be Neurodivergent. But earlier this year I was diagnosed with Autism. They also referred me for ADHD, which I'm pending full assessment for, but they had about an 80% confidence level that I do also have ADHD.

So that's how my mind works. My insanely strong moral code. My inability to give into unethical actions, or let things go by that cause significant harm to people. The way I understand things. There were things the assessor pointed out that I hadn't noticed about myself. Like how I play with my necklace or rings subconsciously, as a sign of anxiety. My lack of direct eye contact. I don't always engage in conversation, but I will ask detailed questions on topics because I need to understand them at a deeper level. When I'm struggling to take something in, that might have come as a shock, I might overreact or go completely silent. Because I don't know how to process that, and I need time to do so. I am passionate about things that interest me, but just cannot get going on things that don't. Everything is about goals. I am obsessed with being efficient but give myself way too much to do.

Finally, I understood, reading a report all about myself from these incredible psychologists. The puzzle was complete. Even down to why I feel it is more of a struggle as I get older. Learning who I am and where I fit into the world has meant I have been able to achieve some amazing things!

- I have 3 biological kids and 2 step kids. Life is busy!
- I have an epic husband. 🩶

- I have my own business.
- I have cats which I love, and they give the best cuddles!
- I am able to foster cats, most often mums with kittens which is just so amazing to be able to do.
- I've held a position on the CIPD Thames Valley Committee for 4 years now where I get to organise events for HR Professionals. I wanted to do that to overcome my fear and anxiety of public speaking and networking. It can still be there, but now I know how to manage it, and I do love the volunteering group! Some amazing people!
- I'm on the board of Broken Spoke – an Oxfordshire based not for profit who make cycling safer for people by training and repairing, as well as recycling bikes!
- I'm launching business number two and drafting a concept for business three!
- I get to work with some of the most amazing startups and SMEs through my HR and Health & Safety Consulting.
- I also have an epic Osteopath who has taught me where my stress sits in my body and has helped me become less tense and more mobile. On my first visit, I was tense everywhere, even my jaw!
- I get to work with some awesome bigger businesses through my collaborative group MOCHA – focused on leadership development and psychological safety in the workplace.

- I have met some amazing people on this journey, and I am grateful to everyone who took the time to offer free advice, support and promoted #collaborationovercompetition

Autism is tiring some days. But it can also be quite amazing. It gives me the fire to get so much done, so quickly. It gives me the ability to think differently and come up with concepts that could turn into great ideas, make things simpler and more efficient. That is what I love doing the most.

How does this all relate to mental health?

Because with conditions like Autism and ADHD, there is a huge stigma still attached. As I write this, I have seen posts this week referring to a study claiming to have "found a cure for Autism". Like it's a disease. Like it's wrong and needs to be changed. It's not cancer. And it's not harming anyone. It's just how I think, and see, and feel. What's worse is the study claimed to have cured two people. Two. Because apparently that's enough data to prove anything.

Actually, all that happened was these poor people were conditioned, and tortured into thinking that there was something wrong with them and that they needed fixing. That is exactly what Autistic people have been masking for so long. Those "naughty" children who were too loud. Those "quiet" children who needed to speak up more. What does that "conditioning" do to their mental health? How do they grow up to be well adjusted adults who can cope with the pressure of life when everything feels wrong?

People with Autism typically live 10-20 years less than those who are Neurotypical. That's pretty significant. Our stress threshold is lower in many ways, but we have become so good at masking that we can take on more stress than most. We just feel it mentally and physically to the point where it shortens our lives. I consider myself incredibly fortunate to have the support network that I have. To have come through what I did and learn who I am. I don't think many people get to do that.

So what are we all going to do about it?

Well, what we should do and what we will do I'm sure are very different. But let's remember a few basic things, shall we? We're all human. We all have hopes and dreams. We all have baggage. So, let's just be kind. Being Neurodivergent is perfectly fine. Being gay, trans, gender neutral, female, male, grey, old, Gen Z, Black, Asian or whatever else is perfectly fine. Be a fu**ing Giraffe if you want to be! Having bright pink hair is perfectly fine. Having tattoos. Having piercings. Who friggin' cares, and why?!

What's not fine is being a turd and hurting others. Physically or mentally. Don't get me started on school rules and the mental health problems they cause with their insistence on conformity to the extent of completely squashing any form of personality at all!

Don't troll. Don't correct everyone for every spelling mistake. You look like an inconsiderate twit. Some people's first language isn't English. If they spell incorrectly on Facebook, who does it hurt? Instead of correcting their spelling, why not tell them they made a great effort, but it's spelled x not y. Maybe English is their first language, but they didn't get a great education. Maybe they are dyslexic. Don't stick in people's minds for being a troll. Stick in their minds for doing good things.

Erm, so what's the grand plan?

I have no interest in having money for money's sake. To sit there in a bank, or to buy things I don't need. My first business will fund my second, and so on. Yes, I want to live comfortably, mortgage free. I want my kids to have a bit of a head start and I would like to make sure they see a bit of the world. But my desire to make more money is so that I can invest that money into other services that make life a bit better for people.

My HR consultancy is people solutions focused. We work with good business owners who want to make sure they look after their people. By aligning HR strategies and business goals, making policies simple and easy to understand and taking out the complexity that a small business simply does not need, we foster positive work cultures that drive natural growth.

Extending that expertise to Health & Safety partners nicely too and comes hand in hand for scientific business which are a large part of my customer base. They have some tight requirements and often wear too many hats. I help take a few of those hats off their busy heads.

Business number two is launching soon! A consultancy startup accelerator that will equip aspiring consultants with the tools and knowledge they need to succeed. Drawing on our collective experience, we'll handle the administrative heavy lifting, allowing you to focus on building your brand and client base. From business setup and website design to financial management and business coaching, we will provide a comprehensive support system. Unlike traditional franchises, our model empowers you to own your business without hefty upfront costs. In just 12 months, you'll be well-positioned to establish a thriving consultancy.

To those who are reading this, I want to leave you with a simple message: Embrace your journey with all its ups and downs. Don't be afraid to take risks, to make mistakes, and to learn from them. And most importantly, remember that you don't have to do it alone. Seek out opportunities to collaborate, to build meaningful relationships, and to support those around you. In the end, it's not just about where you end up—it's about how you get there and who you bring along with you.

Website: www.oxfordpeoplesolutions.co.uk

LinkedIn: www.linkedin.com/in/sherrywhite1/

CHAPTER 19

By Jennifer Ransdell, M.S., BCC

Six Seconds EQ Practitioner, Leadership

& Emotional Intelligence Coach

The Significance of You

We are facing a loneliness epidemic, severely affecting mental health and well-being worldwide. The magnitude of the persistence of the problem of loneliness is apparent by the added measure in the Gallup Global Emotions 2024 report. The statistics show over one in five adults report feeling lonely. It has become the most significant threat to people's ability to thrive because it amplifies negative emotions and suppresses positive ones. (1)

I suffered through loneliness and isolation through the better half of my childhood. I often found myself struggling with overwhelming negative feelings of sadness, isolation, abandonment, oppression, and being unloved. My story has always had people asking the same question: how did I turn out so normal? I won't lie; those were my life's most challenging years. The resources that significantly increased the odds for my well-being and perseverance came in the form of other people and my ability to build Psychological Capital (PsyCap). Fred Luthans developed the concept in the early 2000s for Organizational Psychology. He defined it as an individual's positive psychological development that prospers from the internal positive resources of hope, efficacy, resilience, and optimism. They spell the acronym Hero and make managing and weathering difficult situations possible. (2) These internal resources fueled my energy to remain determined and motivated to see my life as something worth living for.

Hello, everyone! What a privilege it is to be a part of this book and collaborate with so many other courageous authors for World Mental Health Day!

I hope my story lends support and knowledge to all those who suffer from loneliness and isolation—the knowledge that you are significant in this world and people will always need the gift of you!

***"The privilege of a lifetime is being who you are"*–Joseph Campbell.**

Hope–The Perspective that Lights the Way

What comes to mind when you think of the word hope? I think of hope as a positive feeling that holds the belief something good will happen. It allows us to not dwell on negative feelings by keeping a positive mindset that anticipates something brighter in the future. It is one of the four positive psychological constructs that comprise Psychological Capital. In my opinion, it is the most drawn-upon psychological resource when life becomes unbearable. It is what prayers are full of. It is the resource that mentally helps fuel the belief that we can emerge triumphant in our fight. However, as adversities increase, the ability to hold onto hope becomes increasingly more difficult.

As it would be for me when I continued to experience traumatic death and loss in my young life. Within three and a half years, my youngest brother and I lost our entire family of loved ones. Starting at age seven, I lost my mom in a horrific drunk-driving accident in which my brothers and I were also involved. A little over a year later, my mom's entire family disappeared from our lives with no explanation. I later found out my dad kept them away. Their absence was extremely difficult for me. It intensified my loneliness and filled me with anger and confusion over their disappearance. I had been so close to my maternal grandmother and great-grandmother. It was a tough time for me because I lost the rest of my maternal nurturing. Two years later, at age eleven, I lost my eight-year-old brother to a brain aneurysm. Like the death of my mom, I was with my brother when he died. We were sharing a bed on a camping trip. I get choked up over the memory of him waking up from sleep and crying over his head hurting. I remember the utter despair I felt four hours later when I couldn't wake him. I felt completely lost and devastated that my maternal family was not at his funeral. I later found out they were never told about his death.

I can't share my story without telling you that after my mom's death, I convinced myself that I had imagined the car collision before it happened. I later learned that this was a normal response to grief for a child my age (3). I didn't have someone to help me with my grief which caused this belief to become a debilitating phobia of death, believing that my thoughts could cause others to die. This fear dominated my mind for years before it finally let go.

After experiencing those traumatic losses and being forced to face harsh realities, the fighter in me kicked in. The ability to hope became a testament to my inherited strength. I was determined to succeed from a young age, no matter the challenge. I vividly remember learning to ride my first big bike—a red Schwinn 3-speed. I practiced every day, driven by the desire to master it. The hope that I could succeed gave me a sense of control; it fueled my motivation and provided determination to keep going. Hope became the positive force that boosted my well-being, strengthened my resilience, and reinforced my belief that I could get through this.

***"You never know how strong you are until being strong is your only choice."*–Bob Marley.**

Efficacy–The Belief You Can Succeed

Hope brings the positivity that encourages us to push through challenges, but what fuels our belief that we can succeed? This is where the following construct of Psychological Capital comes in: efficacy. Developed by Bandura, self-efficacy is our faith in our ability to produce a desired outcome in any task or challenge. It gives us the confidence that drives our effort and persistence to overcome these obstacles. (2) Building self-efficacy was essential; I needed to trust in my ability to navigate the hurdles that stood in the way of my continued development and well-being.

I drew from a few essential resources contributing to my belief that I could weather my environment successfully. One of the most profound was the healing power of compassion. After my mom's death and my dad's subsequent remarriage, I found myself in a hostile, loveless environment that deepened my loneliness. Struggling with anger and questioning my purpose, I felt guilty for complaining when others faced worse hardships. This internal struggle shifted my focus from my grief to understanding others' suffering, revealing the transformative power of compassion. The impact of extending an external lens to encompass others' feelings led me to see how our suffering diminishes. Knowing that others endured even greater hardships gave me the confidence to face my challenges. I developed a heightened awareness of others' struggles, which helped cultivate my greatest superpower, empathy.

I was raised Catholic, and even from a young age, my belief in God was instrumental to my growth and well-being. He was my constant companion during all that loss; his presence was my only comfort. My deep belief in God gave me the confidence that I could succeed. He helped me understand I had a purpose in life; my life was his gift, and I would one day experience the happiness of being me. I just needed to wait, even though waiting felt like serving a prison sentence.

Another crucial factor in building and strengthening my self-efficacy was drawing on the foundation my mom and her family provided from birth until her death. The early years of a child's life, particularly between birth and age five, are vital for brain development. During this time, genetic and environmental influences shape the child's brain, with parent-child interactions playing a pivotal role in fostering well-being and social competence (4). My relationship with my mom and maternal family continuously reminded me of my identity and origins. Their nurturing presence and the strong genes I inherited significantly shaped my personality and resilience. I incorporated this legacy into my efficacy, which became a powerful tool in every challenge I faced. Additionally, I learned later that my great-grandmother's lineage traced back to the Magna Carta, which reinforced the sense of fighting spirit and resilience that I felt in my veins.

***"The harder the struggle, the more glorious the triumph."*–Swami Sivananda.**

Resilience–The Strength that Fuels Endurance

What enables us to endure hardships, especially when change seems unlikely? This is where resilience—the most crucial construct of

Psychological Capital—comes into play. Resiliency keeps us going when hope, efficacy, and optimism are low (5). It allows us to bounce back and grow stronger from negative experiences (2). While our resilience builds each time we successfully rebound from adversity, we also need other resources to support our mental and physical stamina.

Even though I had become stronger from constantly bouncing back, my mental health and well-being were wearing down. I am incredibly grateful for the people God placed in my life during this time; their presence bolstered my resilience and contributed to my mental health and well-being. Enduring the emotional strain of loneliness throughout my teenage years was highly challenging, especially as an extrovert who thrived on connection. We all share a universal need to feel seen and valued, and the people who showed up for me were the gifts that made all the difference. Their love and support encouraged my resilience and helped me feel my purpose. I would be remiss not to acknowledge the one person who consistently provided the light I needed to manage the darkness—she was the mom I had been missing all those years – her name was Pearl.

Another resource that bolstered my resilience was my continued development of Emotional Intelligence. Although I couldn't change what was happening around me, I discovered that I had the power to limit its impact by enhancing my emotional literacy. According to Six Seconds, emotional literacy is simply identifying and understanding feelings accurately (6). As I began reflecting on people's behaviors and their emotional drivers, I realized that the difficulties I faced weren't about me.

This understanding was instrumental in strengthening my resilience. It empowered me to feel I was in control of choosing how I wanted to feel rather than feeling someone was making me feel something. During this transformative period, I solidified my understanding that I was the only one who controlled my emotions. I didn't fully grasp it then, but this emotional work was pivotal in how my Emotional Intelligence supported my resilience. It was the understanding that I didn't have to accept the transference of other people's emotions onto me. As the saying goes, I could leave it where it belongs, and that was with the other person. I spent many years processing emotions, both mine and others, to help me understand the motivation behind behavior. It increased my resilience and gave me essential knowledge about controlling my feelings. I honed my inner strength as I continued to grow my emotional intelligence.

***"You have power over your mind–not outside events. Realize this, and you will find strength."*–Marcus Aurelius.**

Optimism: The Feeling that Energizes Spirit

One of my top strengths is my zestful energy. I am often told by people they wish they had my energy. I am a WOO in Gallup's Clifton Strengths finder, which means I live for connection and thrive on interacting with others. While WOO is often defined as enjoying "winning others over," I see it as an invitation to share energy and create genuine connections. In a Clifton Strengths webcast series on improving well-being using your

WOO, Dr. Jaclynn Robinson noted how WOOs uniquely energize people by infusing warmth, welcome, and happiness into their interactions. (7) This pretty much sums up why I love connections; I love to spread warmth and happiness.

One of the wonders of this energy is that it's full of optimism, the fourth positive construct in our Psychological Capital. Optimism is often seen as a by-product of hope, efficacy (confidence), and resilience (5). Some say optimism pairs naturally with being hopeful and confident. Still, I see a crucial difference: Hope and confidence are feelings that our brain helps us believe, shining inwardly, while optimism is felt in the heart and shines inward and outward. It becomes infused in our soul's energy!

Maybe it's the loss of loved ones or the profound impact others have had on my well-being, but I deeply understand the value of people and connection. I believe optimism helps spread appreciation and makes connections more meaningful. It also gives us the courage to be vulnerable. Someone once asked why I look for meaning in everything, and I thought, if I'm not searching for meaning, then what's the purpose of living? Optimism helps us continually understand our purpose in life.

When I share a warm smile and good morning with people while riding my bike, I experience the ease of how optimism creates mutual positive synergy. Most often, I receive the same warmth and greeting in return. I then see the happiness that starts to spread across people's faces. It is full of optimism that shows how meaningful connection is.

Optimism is an essential tool that allows me to connect and build trust with others instantly. It's one of my superpowers and a big part of my energy. One way that I fuel my optimism is by practicing my spirituality. It gives me an underlying sense of our connection and role in the universe. One of the most meaningful compliments that made my heart smile came from a dear friend and colleague who said I was the most authentic person she ever knew. I believe optimism helps bring out many meaningful qualities and allows me not to be afraid of being vulnerable in my connections.

***"The meaning of life is to find your gift. The purpose of life is to give it away."* – Pablo Picasso.**

Meaningful Takeaways

***"It's your reaction to adversity, not adversity itself, that determines how your life's story will develop."* —Dieter F. Uchtdorf.**

If there is one thing life has taught me, it's this: we all suffer hardships throughout our lives. As we navigate life's journey, our challenges provide us with knowledge and strength that help us continue to grow and prosper. One of the most critical ways to prosper is through meaningful connections. Our ability to share emotions with others is one of life's greatest gifts that makes us better people. There's a profound sense of validation in being seen, supported, and understood by someone else—an affirmation that resonates profoundly and reminds us we are not alone. I wouldn't have been able to thrive mentally during my teen years without the support and love of others. My psychological strength was rooted in knowing there were people in my life, both past and present, who genuinely loved me. Supportive people around us are essential during difficult times that challenge us mentally.

I'll illustrate this with my own experience: When I'm overwhelmed by challenges, my instinct is to retreat and isolate myself, believing I lack the energy to support others while managing my difficulties. However, I've found that withdrawing doesn't rejuvenate me. Instead, I often miss out on the positive interactions that uplift and energize me.

Finally, I want to emphasize we are much more capable than we know ourselves to be. Some instances during my childhood made me feel like I couldn’t manage anymore. It was profoundly empowering to realize that I could control my internal thoughts and choose how I perceive and think about situations. When we invest in self-work—particularly in understanding and processing our emotions—we empower ourselves profoundly. This work is not just about managing emotions but about recognizing the strength and resilience we already possess. By tuning into our feelings, we gain clarity, self-awareness, and the ability to confidently navigate life’s challenges. Through self-discovery and emotional intelligence, we connect with ourselves and others, creating a foundation for more fulfilling and purposeful lives.

I am a devoted lifelong learner who loves meeting new people and sharing life experiences. I've been blessed with many beautiful connections that have fueled my ability to live with purpose. Becoming a Six Seconds Certified EQ Practitioner has been the highlight of my year, adding significant value to my personal life and coaching practice. I’m passionate about helping people make meaningful connections because relationships are at the heart of our well-being. I coach millennial leaders to become HEROs in building connective cultures that allow people to thrive.

You can get in touch by:

Linktree: www.linktr.ee/leadershipinthemoment

LinkedIn: www.linkedin.com/in/leadershipinthemoment/

References:

(1) www.gallup.com/analytics/349280/gallup-global-emotions-report.aspx

(2) www.positivepsychology.com/psychological-capital-psycap/

(3)www.aacap.org/AACAP/Families and Youth/Facts for Families/FFF- Guide /Children-And-Grief-008.aspx

(4) www.developingchild.harvard.edu/resources/inbrief-science-of-ecd/

(5) www.mindtools.com/aocqqad/what-is-psychological-capital

(6) www.6seconds.org/2023/07/13/enhance-emotional-literacy/

(7)www.gallup.com/cliftonstrengths/en/398237/how-to-improve-your-wellbeing-with-woo.aspx

CHAPTER 20

(Almost) Everything I never wanted anyone to know

By Lauren White

Trauma-informed Coach, Mental Health Trainer, and Professional Declutter & Organiser

Nothing to see here

I talk about mental health a lot. Not my own, obviously. Because *I'm fine.*

'I'm fine' could be used to sum up my approach to my own mental health for decades. There are labels, statistics and pathologies for everything I've experienced in my life. Everything you have too. But even if we've somehow experienced the exact same things, we haven't experienced them in the exact same ways.

You are unique. I am unique. But we are not alone.

I chose to write this, but I don't really want to. I don't want you to know anything, to have any power over me, or to misunderstand. I don't want to lose control.

The kicker is, trying not to be defined by the things that happened *to* me, ignoring them and stuffing them down, meant they seeped into every fibre of my being. I became defined by keeping their silence. I became defined by their impact on my body and my mind.

I also became utterly lost in other people's versions and ideas of me. My world and sense of self was utterly jumbled.

Starting strong

By the time I was 18, I'd amassed significant traumatic experiences and more internal cracks than a desert in a dry spell. This included physical and sexual assault, isolation and loneliness, self-harm, suicidal thoughts, and multiple bereavements. I was a smoker, had a dangerous relationship with alcohol and drugs, had disordered eating - including binge eating and extreme dieting - and had zero self-esteem. Next up, I walked into a long-term abusive relationship with a man older than myself.

I was still 'fine'. None of these things mattered. I'm a high achiever. So I kept amassing, and I kept going.

I didn't know *where* I was going, but I knew I needed to get the hell out of where I was. Over the next decade or two, I was out of the frying pan and into the fire so many times I began to think I was made of Teflon. But I wasn't.

Working 9 to 5 *(is for lightweights)*

Despite everything I had and would experience, one of the most significant things I lost myself to was 'rise and grind' culture. I never wanted to be known as anything other than capable, reliable and fun. So I immersed myself in work, never said no, and kept a packed diary.

After a particularly unpleasant break up, I was left sofa-surfing and desperately unhappy. I didn't want people to know I'd been so stupid as to let this happen, so I pushed them away and didn't allow myself to feel anything.

I booked a 'fuck you' holiday. Which was great – until I contracted a gut parasite that would dictate my health forever after. I was incredibly, incredibly unwell. And incredibly, incredibly not interested in doing anything about it.

At the same time, a member of the Senior Leadership Team at work told me I was good 'within a framework', but not outside of one. I liked that a framework provided rules to be judged by. Performing to someone else's liking was a good thing – I'd go to any level to get positive feedback and try to find value in myself that way. But I knew I could and did think and act both in and outside of the box.

This thinly veiled insult was part of a painful constructive dismissal attempt after I challenged why, when I was doing so well against ever changing goalposts, I didn't have parity with less experienced, less qualified, male colleagues.

I crumbled inward, a husk of a person, brittle, broken and terribly sad. Feeling humiliated, I cracked on and started a new chapter. I threw myself into a new stressful job and took on studies and voluntary positions, often exploring things that had happened to me – never admitting that I was searching for help.

As I walked into more workplaces, often with good people and bad cultures, I increasingly found myself feeling like a burnt out car abandoned in the woods. Once shiny and useful, now empty and unable to go.

Externally, I was fine. Internally, the cracks were getting wider and deeper.

By no means has my life been solely a ball of misery. I've had LOADS of fun, met tonnes of amazing people and done incredible things. I've even fallen in love (and now have the most wonderful, supportive, hype man of a partner). I'm grateful for so much.

One of the most stirring experiences of my life was a three-week trip travelling around Hawaii with one of my closest friends. I felt in constant awe of the stunning scenery and in complete connection with nature, the Earth - the universe! At the time, my friend and I lived in different countries and she left almost a day before me. After she'd gone, I broke down sobbing. I didn't want to go back to my life.

I knew I had to make huge changes. And I did. But they weren't the right ones.

Out of my head and into my body

When I got back, I began to make my plans for change. My body, as it turned out, had its own plans.

I started feeling drained. Like I'd woken up one day and started running ultramarathons without any prep. Beyond exhausted and aching all the time, I sustained muscle and tendon injuries without clear cause and had my worst gut flare since the original incident years before.

Still, I moved to a new place, in a new city. I took on new career challenges. I rescued multiple cats. I took on more voluntary positions. I threw myself into new things. I was determined to make friends, to see and do all the things. Unfortunately, I was no longer holding it together. The cracks opened up and great chunks of me came apart.

There were times my whole body was so rigid and locked that I couldn't physically get out of bed. My legs hurt so much I could barely shuffle to the toilet. My left arm no longer worked. I was frequently confused and unable to articulate myself. Everything I ate caused all kinds of problems. My insomnia was in a new realm of indescribable misery. I had shooting pains, nerve pain, gnawing, aching, and throbbing pains. Fainting episodes, low mood, wild swings in body temperature, and random shakes. Everything was screaming on red alert, all the time. It was disorientating. My mind had always been one for racing, but this was Formula 1. My body was doing everything in its power to stop me from carrying on as I was.

Despite this, I carried on. I forced myself to go to work. I'd often get there late – but I got there. Stressed about being late. Working in a high-performance environment that showed no mercy. I used sugar like a drug, fuelling me through painful, shattering afternoons – then crashed into thousands of pieces every evening.

After an incredibly long, painful, frustrating - and expensive - number of years (including time where I didn't seek help, believing I could manage alone), I was diagnosed with several chronic and immune illnesses, including fibromyalgia.

I mention fibromyalgia specifically as it's the thing I talk about the least. It isn't the end of a diagnosis: it's the beginning of many more. It also groups things previously diagnosed (for example, TMJ, Raynaud's, tinnitus, frozen shoulder, rashes, vestibular migraines – I could go on) under the same umbrella. It's both the cause of anything wrong with you from that point onward and something dismissed as not worthy of investigation.

I was told to take amitriptyline and be on my way. Owing to an earlier horrendous experience with SSRIs and a long, complicated history (from age nine) trying to combat extreme period problems, I decided that tackling symptoms, not causes, wasn't going to work for me this time round.

I read absolutely everything I could and spoke to hundreds of people. I researched clinics, treatments, holistic and alternative medicines. I looked at symptoms both individually and as a whole, and reluctantly began working away on them.

Pilates helped put me back in my body. It used movements I'd already begun doing on my own before starting - things that helped with specific pains or issues. I focused on my breathing, which led me to undertake a variety of breathing practices, spreading some minor relief throughout my body. I started to explore myself and what I wanted, getting back into coaching and delving into decluttering and organising from a professional perspective. I actively worked on resting. I made friends with my vagus nerve and took a serious look at my gut health.

I learned about trauma and mental health because I wanted to help myself as well as others.

It's important to note, I've had various treatments and currently take 100+ supplements per week. I'm still in pain daily. This isn't everything. But it's a basis.

However, then, I was still in superhero mode, doing everything all at once instead of pacing myself. Things were going reasonably well. Until I started having agonising incidents unlike any I'd had previously.

Did I seek help? My most recent interactions with doctors confirmed that help was not available. (It is - don't fall into the same trap!) I'd learnt loads – but not yet that I can't handle everything solo. And that no one is supposed to.

For over a year, these incidents increased in pain, severity and frequency. Their impact was huge, causing me to need an increasing amount of time off work. Instead of taking time off, I worked from home, so I could wail in agony, sweat, cry and be sick in private (except for my cats, who have no boundaries – especially when it comes to bathrooms).

Having my gallbladder removed finally saw me change my life in the way I'd needed all along.

After having surgery to remove the 'ghastly specimen' on a Thursday afternoon, I gave myself until Sunday to be well enough to do the things that needed doing at home, to start the online course I'd signed up for and to go for a little walk. I planned to force and bully myself to do these things, as usual.

On Friday morning, less than 24 hours post surgery, a colleague asked if I 'wanted to check something over'. In that moment - wild eyed, greasy haired, in pain, bloated and confused - I knew that if I said yes, I was confirming forever that work was 'it' - the number one priority. That other things and people weren't it. That I wasn't it. I finally chose myself. I declined.

Being the calm *and* the storm

My therapist asked, 'is your life chaotic, or are you chaotic?' Obviously, the answer was my life. But I decided to sense-check it.

My partner said, 'I don't think you're chaotic at all.' A pause. 'You are a bit like, *I just started another course, I need to drop this off shortly, we need to pick that up later, I'm just popping to help my neighbour with something, I've found a new recipe for tonight, look at this cool place I've booked us, and I need to read this book by 5pm today.*' I canvassed a few other opinions, receiving similar responses with varying levels of politeness. In short, yes, I was chaotic.

I thought living life to the fullest meant saying yes to everything and everyone. I'd subscribed to the idea of being 'always-on' for so long that I thought it was the only way. It left me in a whirlwind of confusion. Always chasing; never getting ahead.

One way I've always found peace is by Sorting Shit Out.

Just this morning, my Mum texted me: 'I remember how tidy and organised your room was and your control of things. Very unusual in one so young.' If that doesn't scream trying to make order out of chaos, I don't know what does.

I often find myself impacted by my surroundings. If I'm stressed, the walls close in. Sometimes, I see a bare spot in, let's say my lounge, and have a feeling of spaciousness - something allowing for growth and expansion. Other times, I see it as a void that needs to be filled immediately. I can feel the need to remove ten things right now, or to fill every nook and cranny until they're overflowing.

We relate to our stuff in a multitude of different ways. Perhaps you keep your Gran's fine China tea set because it was your Gran's. You don't like or use it and it's taking up precious space. But you keep it. Or you want to get rid of the clothes you bought on a whim that never fitted properly. Guilt about fast fashion waste stops you from taking action, so they sit and fester, clouding you with bad energy.

Maybe you dread waking up to hundreds of emails and thousands of social notifications every morning but are resigned to it because 'we live in a digital world'. Having stuff can make us feel secure. Removing it can make us feel threatened. (People panic buying toilet roll and hand sanitiser during lockdown, for example.)

I had always found it cathartic to have a clear out, to start afresh, to make sure the things that New Me needed were easily accessible. Now I know it's about that – but also so much more than that. Because these are just further unnecessary layers. Layers that we can shed, once we build our resilience and flex our own opinion muscles. We are not our minds. Our minds are only a part of us. They're a tool for us to use. If we don't intervene to set the direction, they'll run us – and we might not like where we end up.

I had been living my life as one big To-Do list, wondering why I never made a dent in it. Not having time to savour what I was doing because I was too focused on finishing it and getting on to the next thing. My mindset was constantly 'if I can just get through this week, things will start to work out.'

Unravelling is generally seen as a bad thing when it comes to mental health. I say quite the opposite, once we unravel all the knots we've tied ourselves in, we're able to build a life we love living.

Have you ever seen an old painting being restored? The process usually begins with a gentle dusting of the top layer, going on to carefully dab and clean away built-up grime and dirt until, eventually, the bright, shining original is uncovered in all its colourful glory. I thought that I was beyond repair. But I was never broken to begin with. I was always there, intact and glorious.

I've carried on uncovering myself, decluttering my thoughts and my space, taking on challenges and qualifications that have meaning and reward for me. I've found confidence in the skills and experience I already have, and ways to help people that aren't at my own expense.

Humans are meaning machines. We create and attach it everywhere. People whispering on the bus? They must be talking about us. Someone doesn't instantly reply to our message? They're mad at us. We take external meaning and make it internal. But when it comes to the bigger picture, to purpose – we look externally, searching everywhere but ourselves. Finding a cure for cancer would be hugely purposeful, right? But kids on a cancer ward will forever remember the clown who entertained them as they underwent treatment. Isn't being a clown then profoundly purposeful?

I recently made a HUGE list of things I want to do. As I started planning when I'd do them, I realised I don't want to do them all. Some are just nice-to-haves. Some are other people's ideas. What I do want is to make sure I have enough time to just sit quietly in my garden, feeling the sun on my face and my cats rubbing against my legs while a cup of tea warms my hands. Now that's living.

Make space for you

Life hacks and overnight changes were sticking plasters on a gaping wound. Forcing myself made things worse. Imagine scrubbing at the painting being restored. Rather than removing the layers quicker, it would likely tear the original, requiring even more work to restore it. I wanted change and I wanted it fast. Because of that, nothing I did lasted. I didn't realise that change is like a revolution: it *doesn't* happen overnight. Organising and action take place everyday and, over time, build to something bigger.

Now I have fun and I'm happy.

If I don't move around enough, my joints swell and my muscles and tendons stiffen and cause unbearable agony. If I move around or take on too much, the same thing happens. I'm learning a very visceral lesson about balance. I don't always get it right and it's not always clear-cut. But everyday I'm learning.

And I know I'm not alone.

- Almost half of the UK have a long-standing health problem or chronic illness that impedes their day-to-day life (ONS).
- 1 in 3 women experience physical and/or sexual abuse in their lifetime (WHO).
- 1 in 4 people in England experience mental health problems every single year. 1 in 4 people globally experience mental health problems in their lifetime (Mind / WHO).
- Around a quarter to 1 in 5 working adults experience burnout symptoms (Mental Health UK / Mckinsey Health).
- 1 in 8 young people have self-harmed in the UK in the last year (Harmless).

- 92% of people who hoard have at least one other mental health disorder (Hoarding UK).
- Every single one of us will experience bereavement at some point in our lives.

I could go on. Instead, I'll say this: You're not a statistic. You're not the things that have happened to you. You're not alone.

The ideal time to work on yourself is when you're feeling strong and happy. But the best time is *right now.* Start where you are, work with what you've got, celebrate as you go. Remember:

1. **You don't have to believe other people's opinions of you.** You can't control them and they're really none of your business. Focus on how you relate to yourself then radiate outwards.

2. **Ignore the false sense of urgency. It takes as long as it takes.** Uncover the layers and emerge from the roles you've taken on. Enjoy the exploration. Doing something more than nothing everyday *is* change.

3. **Happiness comes from doing things that make you happy.** It's not some elusive state you can chase down or go and set up camp in. Happiness and purpose are inextricably linked.

4. **Make your heart sing. Create joyful expressions of yourself.** Clutter is stuff that doesn't have a home or a purpose, whether in your thoughts, habits, phone or home. Our spaces can be beautiful reflections of who we are.

5. **Safety is essential for healing to take place.** You are the longest relationship you will ever be in. Any work you do to make yourself your own safe space is worth the time, cringe and effort to do so.

I didn't write this chapter in a linear way, against both convention and advice. I wrote things as they surfaced, then stitched and wove them together to create meaning. Sometimes we need to sift through everything to find the parts we want to keep – and the parts we want to let go of.

If you want to sift through the things getting in your way - physically or mentally - to uncover what you want and remove what you don't, I'd love to help.

Website: www.unjumble.uk

LinkedIn: www.linkedin.com/in/laurenhwhite/

CHAPTER 21

By Magdalena Zbyszynska

Self-Leadership for Wellbeing: A Journey to True Self-Alignment

The concept of leadership is well-established in the corporate world, with countless theories and approaches to foster employee engagement. Inspirational quotes abound, yet statistics show that workplace culture often negatively impacts mental health, suggesting that despite the wealth of available wisdom, many people are not thriving. My interest in leadership grew subtly, through observing how people evolve at work and how their personal choices ripple into other areas of their lives. As I practised the principles of leadership, I noticed their profound impact beyond the workplace, particularly in helping individuals develop healthier, more fulfilling lives. This realisation led me to a deeper focus on self-leadership—the psychological and personal dimension of leading oneself.

In this chapter, I invite you to join me to explore the various dimensions of self-leadership and its impact on mental health and well-being. Through personal stories, client experiences, and practical lessons, we'll delve into how self-leadership can transform our lives, helping us achieve true alignment and fulfilment. Whether you're just beginning your journey or looking to deepen your practice, this chapter offers valuable insights and tools to enhance your self-leadership skills for a more fulfilling life.

The Power of Self-Leadership

There was a time in my life when I felt like I was drifting, constantly reacting to whatever life threw at me. I would wake up each day feeling like I was merely going through the motions, ticking off tasks on a to-do list, but never feeling truly fulfilled. I made decisions based on what I thought others expected of me, rather than what resonated with my values. And when I wanted to stand up for myself, of course, I did the opposite, often ending with unexpected outcomes. This inner detachment left me feeling empty, anxious, and unsure of my path, yet my dreams were big. At the same time, being in this internal battle with myself contemplating my existence and its purpose led to irrational decisions.

It wasn't until I stumbled upon the concept of self-leadership that things began to change. The idea of leading my own life—of taking intentional control of my thoughts, emotions, and actions—was both freeing and frightening. But as I began to explore this concept, I realised it was the missing piece I had been searching for. Slowly, through trial and error, I started to implement self-leadership into my daily life. I learned to align my decisions with my true values and aspirations, and over time, this transformation led me to the work I do today.

Life Without Self-Leadership: A Silent Struggle

Imagine waking up every day feeling like you're on a treadmill, constantly moving but never getting anywhere. You're busy, yet there's a nagging sense that something is missing. Your days are filled with tasks and responsibilities, but they lack meaning and fulfilment. Decisions feel more like reactions to external pressures than choices made from a place of inner clarity. It seems an excellent idea to blame others rather than taking responsibility for our own actions😉.

When we don't practice self-leadership, life can feel like it's happening *to us rather* than *for us*. We may find ourselves caught in a cycle of stress and dissatisfaction, chasing goals that don't truly resonate with us. We might struggle with indecision, feel disconnected from our true selves, and constantly seek validation from others, all while knowing deep down that something needs to change. Forgetting too often we are the authors of our daily narrative. Take a moment here for a quick reflection. What narrative have you created today? Write it down and read it again… This is the reality for many people, and it was my reality too—until I discovered the power of self-leadership.

Embracing Self-Leadership: Your Path to Empowerment

Self-leadership is not just a buzzword; it is a fundamental component of mental health and well-being. When we lead ourselves effectively, we are better equipped to navigate life's challenges, make informed decisions, and maintain a sense of balance and fulfilment. It is the practice of becoming the leader of your own life—making decisions that align with your deepest values and aspirations. It empowers us to create value in our lives by engaging in activities that resonate with our true selves, thereby fostering a deeper sense of purpose and satisfaction.

Habits create emotional distance from distractions because your focus is strengthened.

But how do you start this journey of self-leadership? It begins with awareness. By cultivating self-awareness, we gain insights into our strengths, weaknesses, and motivations. This awareness allows us to align our actions with our true selves, leading to greater authenticity and inner peace. It also helps us recognise and overcome limiting beliefs and behaviours that may hinder our progress.

Introducing the Self-Awareness Journey: A Practical Exercise

To guide you on this journey, I've developed an awareness-building tool that helps identify factors impacting how we feel and how we can change certain patterns when we commit to continuous learning. This tool is a roadmap for decision-making, a way to gain clarity about where you've been, where you are now, and where you want to go.

Figure 1 Self-Awareness Journey for decision-making process

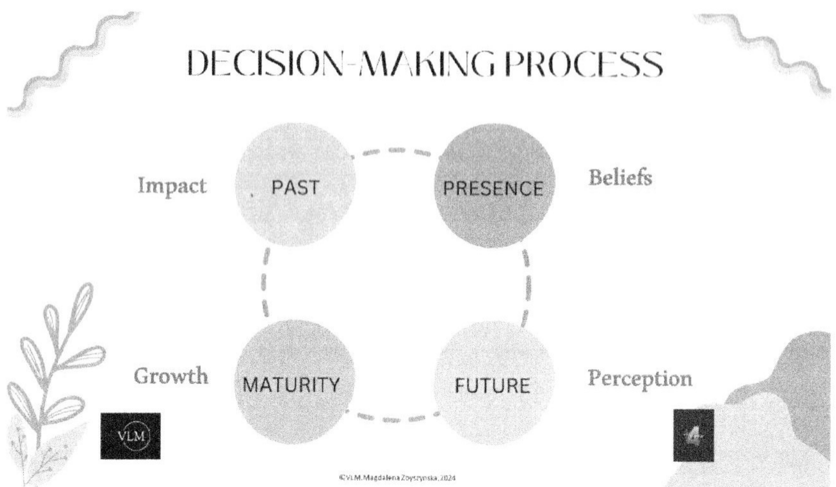

Before we dive into your self-discovery journey, let me share an example of how this exercise might unfold. Imagine Sarah, who identifies *resilience* as a strength from her past and recalls a challenging breakup that left a lasting impact. By mapping out these experiences, Sarah gains clarity on how her past shapes her present and how she can consciously steer her future.

Now, it's your turn.

This exercise is about you—so take this time to focus on yourself, free from distractions or the influence of others. I encourage you to use a dedicated journal for this exercise. Label it 'My Self-Discovery Journal,' and treat it as a sacred space for your thoughts and reflections.

Exercise 1: Your Self-Discovery Journey

1. **Prepare Your Journal:** Divide a page into four squares or draw a table with four columns and label them as follows: Past, Present, Maturity, Future.
2. **PAST:**
    - Think about 2-3 positive strengths or values you have from your past (use one word for each, not a full event or story).
    - Reflect on 2-3 facts or situations from your past that might have hurt you.
3. **PRESENT:**
    - Follow the same format as the "Past" section but relate it to your current life.
4. **FUTURE:**
    - Answer the following questions with as much specificity as possible:
    - What do I want in life? (Avoid general statements like "I want to be happy." Be specific.)
    - How do I want to feel about myself? (Again, avoid generalities. Dive deep into what, for example, happiness or success means for you.)
5. **MATURITY:**
    - Look back at the negative statements from your Past and Present sections. For each statement, rate your emotional attachment on a scale from 0 (disconnected/not attached anymore) to 6 (strongly connected and affected).

- Use these scores to assess areas of your life where emotional attachments may still be influencing your decisions. The higher the score, the more likely it is that emotional attachment is guiding your choices and/or behaviours.

6. **FUTURE VISUALISATION:**

- Read through your answers in the Future column. Close your eyes, straighten your back, and take five deep, slow breaths.
- Visualise yourself in the state you've described. Imagine how it feels to live in alignment with your purpose and vision. Write down any emotions or insights that arise from this visualisation.

What This Exercise Reveals

- **Maturity:** Higher scores in your emotional attachment ratings indicate areas where you may need to work on detaching and making more rational, less emotionally driven decisions. These are areas for growth and development.
- **Future:** Your answers to "What do I want in life?" represent your *Purpose*, while "How do I want to feel about myself?" represents your *Vision.*

This exercise is the beginning of your journey toward self-leadership. I encourage you to revisit it every few months to track your growth and see how your answers evolve. Remember, self-leadership is a continuous journey. Let your vision be your drive and allow yourself the grace to grow into the leader of your own life.

My Journey and the Concept of "Toxic Needs"

My journey of self-discovery led me to identify what I call "toxic needs"—deep-rooted, unmet needs from our past that invisibly shape our decisions and actions today. This term emerged from my own experiences, as I grappled with understanding the mechanisms that influenced how I perceived myself and others. The journey was far from easy. It required me to confront painful truths and acknowledge that many of the decisions I made as an adult were driven by these unfulfilled needs from my childhood. Without the right support or environment, these needs can dominate our lives, leading us to make choices that do not serve our true selves. In the long term this can negatively affect our mental health and overall wellbeing.

Elly's Story: The Need for Healthy Attention

Take the story of Elly, for example. She was caught in a cycle of turbulence in her marriage, where arguments had become a daily occurrence. In her mind, her husband was the root of all her problems—he was never enough. She ignored the opinion of others that her choice was not right, and she was convinced that in her case it would be different. And she believed she would change him into a good man. However, as the initial infatuation faded, reality set in, and Elly began to blame her husband for her unhappiness and bouts of depression.

Through her self-discovery work, Elly realised that her decision to marry was not a mature choice, but rather a response to her deep-seated need to feel loved. This need, unmet in her childhood, led her to see her husband through rose-coloured glasses, blinding her to reality. Her childhood had been devoid of the love and support she craved, and when she found a man who showered her with attention, she believed she had found everything she was missing.

It was only after she identified this toxic need and took responsibility for her choices that she found the strength to de-rewire the dynamic in her marriage. Surprisingly for Elly, she received enormous support from her husband in her journey, eventually joining her and discovering again the beauty of love. The experience for both was exploratory and with many failures, however, commitment led them to success and met real life satisfaction.

In Elly's case, the unmet need was for healthy attention—attention that is mature, balanced, and supportive of a person's development. Healthy attention involves communication, knowledge sharing, and inspiration, often neglected because they require deep engagement.

Clark's Story: The Need for Respect and Assertiveness

Another example is Clark, a young graphic designer working in a large team with two leaders and one manager. The manager delegated all authority to the leaders, who, due to their differing personalities, struggled to coordinate effectively. As a result, Clark was often burdened with additional work, staying late to complete tasks that others had neglected. Despite his efforts, his leaders were never satisfied, frequently criticising his work and leaving Clark in a state of constant fear and anxiety.

Clark's attempts to impress his leaders or seek support from his manager only led to more criticism. Yet, the leaders continued to rely on Clark for extra work, taking credit for his efforts without acknowledging his contributions.

The toxic need driving Clark's behaviour was the need for respect and assertiveness. Many of us are raised to be polite, kind, and accommodating, often to the point of suppressing our own needs and desires. These rooted behaviours can leave us measuring our worth through others' opinions, making it difficult to stand up for ourselves as adults, which can lead to a people-pleaser mode. By understanding these toxic needs and how they influence our decisions, we can begin to break free from their hold, allowing us to make choices that truly serve our well-being.

Self-leadership involves recognising these patterns, confronting them, and ultimately transforming them into strengths that guide us toward a more fulfilling life.

Clark resigned from work and found another opportunity where he started to implement the behaviours immediately as he knew it would enable him to be perceived in the way he wanted. In knowing himself better when going for interviews Clark was better prepared with questions to ask his potential new employer. This helped him to define if the culture and leadership approach was focused on people's growth or internal competition.

Ben's Story: The Need for Empathy and Communication

Ben was a manager in a sales company, renowned for his effectiveness in hitting targets and driving his team's performance. His ability to connect with clients and grow sales made him an asset to the management team. As his team consistently delivered outstanding results, Ben's income soared year after year. This financial success fostered a sense of power in Ben, shaping him into a leader who believed in ruling with an iron fist. He saw fear as the ultimate motivator, thinking that by instilling it in his team, they would exceed expectations and, in turn, earn more. "Results matter, not people's feelings," became Ben's motto. He believed that his team should be grateful to him for their financial success.

However, after many years of what seemed like successful leadership, Ben's career took a drastic turn. Despite his impressive results, the management team could no longer ignore the growing number of complaints about his leadership style. Ben was let go. For a long time, he struggled to find another job. The connections he thought were solid friendships, built during luxurious leisure times, vanished when he needed them most.

Through this challenging period, Ben came to a profound realisation: he had grown up in a household where fear was a constant companion, served at every meal. Pain was presented as a necessary tool for growth, and fear was the fuel to push harder. Commands were the norm, leaving no room for Ben's voice or opinions. The ultimate goal in his family was money, as it was seen as the key to respect. The more money one had, the more respect and power they commanded.

The toxic needs that drove Ben—empathy and communication—were glaringly absent in his life. He realised that his upbringing had conditioned him to value results and financial success over human connection and understanding. This epiphany led Ben to a new path. He became a coach for leaders, dedicating his career to teaching the importance of empathy and communication in team management. These core components are now central to his message, as he helps others avoid the mistakes he once made.

These stories are a powerful reminder that the way we feel is not the responsibility of others. It is our accountability to define, understand, and acknowledge these feelings, and to do the necessary work to address them if we want to lead fulfilling, connected lives.

Engagement and Value Creation

A key aspect of self-leadership is awareness. By cultivating self-awareness, we gain insights into our strengths, weaknesses, and motivations. This awareness allows us to align our actions with our true selves, leading to greater authenticity and inner peace. It also helps us to recognise and overcome limiting beliefs and behaviours that may hinder our progress. From my work with clients and observation of others, I see most people expect the results within just the expression of the will to change. Once introduced to the work, unfortunately, many will step back, continuing to "enjoy" a life that does not fully satisfy them.

***How soon "not now" becomes "never"* – Martin Luther**

This quote captures a common struggle: the habit of postponing change. We often convince ourselves that we'll start tomorrow, next week, or when circumstances are more favourable. But the truth is, every time we say, 'not now,' we edge closer to 'never.' This procrastination can quietly erode our potential, leaving our goals and dreams perpetually out of reach. The gap between 'not now' and 'never' can be dangerously small, and it's easy to fall into this trap. The more we delay acting, the more comfortable we become in our current state, even if it's unsatisfying. This is why engagement in the process of change is crucial. It requires us to challenge the instinct to delay, to push past the resistance that whispers, 'later.' Remember, change doesn't happen in some distant future—it begins in the present moment. Each small step we take today moves us further from 'never' and closer to our true potential. It's about making a choice, again and again, to prioritise our growth and well-being over the comfort of the status quo.

Our own engagement to change is key in this journey, not placing expectations on others and further being disappointed that they did not meet our desired outcome. Another way to change your journey is to find a new justification for why "not now". It's your work, not theirs. And let me share with you a secret: it's not so difficult. You only need to give yourself some time and let it be quality time.

When we commit to a practice, we naturally develop a focus on the value we want to create. Rome was not built in one day, so do not put on yourself harsh demands. Build the transformation with small but strongly anchored steps. The change is never about money or circumstances but your mindset and conscious presence. With that attitude, you will be able to create integrity between your thoughts and actions. Can one be trusted if saying one thing and doing another? Not really.

Let me leave you now with a few quick-fix tips, hoping the things I have shared in this chapter will help you to define your better tomorrow.

Daily empowerment routine:

- **Plan your week around your goals.** Planning brings peace and supports self-awareness. Engage your family or a friend in your journey. Discuss your feelings and emotions as you take steps toward your goals. Let them be there for you, just as they are. Communicate the type of support you need—don't assume they know just because they've known you for years. Open communication works wonders.
- **Dedicate 30 minutes a day to a specific task.** 30 minutes is just a fraction of a day's active hours. This is something you can do with your family as well. Silent work, where everyone focuses on their task, whether it's yoga, reading, meditation, or journaling. Document this moment and use it as a reference point.
- **Meditate before sleep.** If you find it hard to find time, adjust your schedule. As a mom, I've changed the clock rule, and you can too. 😉
- **When motivation wanes, countdown 3–2–1—and move forward!**

Contact me:

LinkedIn: www.linkedin.com/in/magdalena-zbyszynska

Website: www.vlmsolution.com

COURAGE

"ONE DAY YOU WILL TELL YOUR STORY OF HOW YOU OVERCAME WHAT YOU WENT THROUGH AND IT WILL BE SOMEONE ELSE'S SURVIVAL GUIDE."

- BRENE BROWN

CHAPTER 22

Glass half empty Martin – The Courageous Journey to Success!

By Caroline Martin

To write, or not to write, that is the question

I have never found it a challenge to share my experiences, that is until now. I have however, wasted endless hours at times worrying that I have said the wrong thing to the wrong person, worrying that I have shared inappropriately and worrying that I have made myself look less of a professional.

I was brought up not to air my dirty laundry in public which has protected me over the decades.

I am generally guarded with whom I have had the courage to share and so even if you have known me for a while, you may know very little unless something has cropped up in a 121 or small gathering. This, right now, is me taking a step forward to change that, coupled with a fear that you… YES YOU… might be that person that deems me less of a professional for doing so.

When I was invited to join this book collaboration I was absolutely delighted. Not only was I going to appear in a second book with another bunch of incredibly inspiring people, but this book is to be launched on World Mental Health Day 2024. Mental wellbeing is a topic very close to my heart.

So why have I been so stuck for the last three months?

My challenge is because firstly, I admire coaches and professionals that openly share what's happening on a regular basis to inspire their audiences, but I have also seen this viewed as a sign of weakness by some. People have even been locked up for not presenting as society's idea of what is 'normal behaviour' so it's hardly surprising that many of us have it hard wired into us not to share the deep stuff, or sometimes any stuff.

Secondly, life is a journey we seldom travel alone. Many of the big things that I have encountered have involved others and I therefore do not believe they are mine to air in the public domain.

Finally, I am afraid, afraid of the public shame that I could bring on to myself and to my family which could fall completely against the purpose of me writing this chapter in the first place.

Contemplating this chapter has awakened my memories of past trauma so vividly that I have re-lived things that I thought were healed.

Contemplating this chapter has conjured up the frank reality that I most certainly do not have everything in life sussed.

Contemplating this chapter has also served to remind me to show gratitude for the staying power of the person I have always been and of the challenges I have yet to overcome.

Obsessive Compulsive Disorder

I have had my own personal troubles through the years, I'm not sure that any of us come through life unscathed. If you have heard any of my stories before you will know that, for decades, I would say that I could write stories for Eastenders! Back then, even though others could see greatness in me and told me that I was doing a fantastic job, my thinking was so negative that I was referred to as 'Glass half empty Martin'. I honestly was not offended by this title as I genuinely believed that life was, and would always be, hard.

I was jealous of what I thought other people's lives were like. I never even considered that they were possibly guarded from sharing stuff that was happening behind closed doors too. The challenges I had were all 100% real events that happened to me and those I love, but I was so caught up in the devastation that I could barely see a single positive thing that life had to offer. I was a victim.

I am not now immune, though I have learned to perceive things differently. I have overcome a lot, but it's not like everything is plain sailing either. My goodness the universe has presented me with some whoppers to manage just whilst contemplating what to focus on in this chapter and so my blocker has definitely not been a lack of potential content.

So when deliberating what to discuss, instead of throwing in the notebook and quitting, which I can assure you I have considered daily, I have reminded myself of why this particular publication is so important to me.

Poor mental health has quite literally killed and seriously injured people that are dear to me.

Yep, you read that right. People that I know have died of suicide and serious mental health issues. I am writing this chapter in desperate hope that if you are injured, something in this book might land for you. The message may or may not come from me but perhaps something in this book might help you towards your goal or even save your life.

My Story

In my early teens I developed anorexia, which was later followed with bulimia, smoking and drinking. In my 20's I still smoked but had more healthy obsessions with swimming and gyming. When I was pregnant with my daughter, I was obsessed with not smoking or drinking, eating the right foods and specifically in the right quantities.

When my daughter was born, she suffered a complication after birth. She stopped breathing a few times which meant she had to be observed every 30 minutes whilst in hospital. I don't have room in this chapter to describe all of the trauma but I will say that the medical staff didn't notice her choking and fighting for breath after she was born.

Once we were finally discharged from hospital, I asked the nurse to check my daughter one more time. The nurse merely glanced at the cot from four meters away and told me she was 'fine'. I felt really silly for asking her to check and we bundled up her tiny body into her car seat and headed home.

On our first night home together, I couldn't sleep, I was going through the samples of nappies and lotions we had been given in hospital and I came across her discharge notes. I realised that the nurse had discharged me with another mother's notes, a mother and baby with zero complications, meaning she had discharged the wrong baby!

Five days later, after complaining that I had been feeling unwell for days, a new midwife recognised that I had developed a severe infection that had been missed by the previous midwife for the preceding days. This and other serious instances with family members having poor medical treatment left me with a feeling that I couldn't trust anyone, not even professionals.

Sleep deprived, juggling my new job as a mum and managing my own illness, I was delirious. This was the start of my next obsession.

4oz water…. I counted the scoops…. 1, 2, 3, 4…. I glanced at the tin, **You will harm your baby if you do not use the correct dosage.** 'Did I count the milk correctly? Did I measure the water properly? I'm not sure. Better start again….'

4oz water…. 1, 2, 3, 4…. 'Did I actually count that? Better start again….'

As a new mum, like many mums, I built our world around her routine which created unconscious checklists for everything. That is something that many people do but, coupled with illness, exhaustion and fear I couldn't remember if the thing I was doing was today or yesterday. I was living in Groundhog Day, exhausted and consumed with fear that something bad would happen. I felt that I couldn't trust anyone to help. The only exception was my mum, who had spotted the issue with her breathing in the first place. I also didn't want anyone knowing that I wasn't coping.

Dummies, nappies, wipes, juice, purse, keys, mobile phone, cooker, straighteners…

Did I check the cooker? I'm not sure? Cooker is off…. What about my straighteners? Do I have my keys or did I put them back down when I came in?

Dummies, nappies, wipes, juice, purse, keys, mobile phone, cooker, straighteners…

Whaaaaat… I can't remember actually checking. I will need to go back in.

Dummies, nappies, wipes, juice, purse, keys, mobile phone, cooker, straighteners…

Arggghhhhhh… Half-way down the road this time, my breathing quickened, and tears started to roll down my face, I turned back.

Getting out was a rarity. When I was finally out and about people would comment at how advanced my baby was and how I made things look so easy. They had no idea of the trauma I was going through internally or what it had taken to show up.

When it was time for her 1-year check we attended the doctor's surgery. I was due to return to work the next day and the nurse asked how I was. I immediately burst into floods of tears. I couldn't trust anyone to look after her. I didn't know how I was going to cope.

Within minutes I was diagnosed with depression and prescribed anti-depressants. A few weeks later, after the medication settled in, I felt flat. It calmed me and everyone around me thought this was a good thing, but I was no longer happy, or sad, or anywhere in between. I was just a shell, going through the motions of life, doing the things that 'Good' mums do and going to work and doing my best there too. I was still checking, rechecking and forgetting, only now I didn't really care so much. I also still felt really rubbish about myself but had no emotions to express that or anything else.

Years later, I was referred to a councillor who diagnosed me with OCD. He set me tasks to not clear up the toys, not wash up before I did anything and not to check my internal lists. Each week, I would arrive at the sessions feeling great, proud of my progress since the last time. He would then ask me a list of questions, digging into absolutely everything. By the end of the session, I was left feeling like all my success for the week were failures and I sobbed all the way home. I'm sure you can imagine what undoing my tidiness also did to the state of my previously beautifully clean and tidy home.

It was shortly after I started counselling that I discovered personal development. I knew that I had somehow lost some great parts of me that I wanted to get back. I knew to do that I needed to get back on the career ladder, but back then this wasn't something you could do part time in the financial services industry, and I didn't want to sacrifice time away from my children.

I was introduced to Arbonne, a network marketing company. The products transformed my skin, which paved the way for my next obsession, which was a healthier one, into skincare and nutrition. People in this phenomenal culture were transforming physically and mentally before my eyes, but the secret I was looking for was not in the ingredients list. When I asked what they were doing they talked about 'reading'. I was resistant to 'self-help' because the encounter with the councillor had only served to make me feel more miserable about myself, but after several months seeing the change in them, I had to try it.

I had always been curious about what makes people successful. How come some people that are extremely technical and highly educated could not reach the success that they desired? How come some people that did really badly at school achieved huge success?

When I started reading books written by highly successful entrepreneurs and business leaders, I realised that these people had thoughts just like I do. I realised that they had challenges just as I do. I realised that they had discovered tools and techniques to overcome the challenges and turn them into successes. This was the start of another obsession; I could feel my brain coming alive again. I wanted to step back into my 11-year-old entrepreneur self that I had left behind in primary school.

I was done with the dead brain. Much to everyone's concern, I ditched the antidepressants, switching them for anything that would give me a positive mental focus. To be clear, I did turn into a loon for a while and so I wouldn't recommend it to anyone else, but I was pleased to feel the emotions, any emotions. Some days I felt extatically happy, some days I felt desperately depressed and unworthy. Every day I felt grateful to feel alive again.

In 2016 I fell upon coaching, completely unplanned. I had separated from the father of my children. On the first weekend alone without my kids, all of my friends were busy, and I didn't know how to spend my time. A free coaching course in London came up on Facebook and I thought it would keep me occupied. I had never done anything outside of work on my own and I was terrified, but not as terrified as the idea of being on my own.

Whilst I was there, I realised that I knew the tools they were teaching from work. I had just never contemplated that people actively set goals outside of the business environment. That weekend course led me to another, where I fell down the rabbit hole in a deep way and discovered Neuro Linguistic Programming, the study of human excellence.

Wow! This was what I had been searching for all my life. Not a book of theory. Not diving into the reasons which became excuses for why I was so stuck. This presented me with practical tools to overcome challenges through modelling success. I had to learn more!

Obsessive, Committed and Driven

Now that I look back, my obsessions were quite comical really and so now if repetitive behaviour kicks in I try to see the funny side and not wallow in self-loathing. Just imagine if it were recorded, me going round and round the house and in and out of the front door. It would probably make a viral TikTok, like Nemo 'We go out, and back in'!

I am also able to see that these were not weaknesses that needed be abolished from my being. In fact, trying to remove them only caused bigger problems.

I would bet money that, even if you cannot see it right now, the things you perceive as your biggest weaknesses hold the keys to your greatest strengths in a different context. In the extreme states, unhealthy obsessions do not serve me but on the flip side to that, the obsession into human behaviour is at the fundamental core of what makes me great at what I do and what drives me to improve every single day.

If you have just started following me you may think 'well it's alright for her isn't it' and that is OK because that's exactly what I would have thought too, maybe you will catch yourself eyerolling too, as I would have done. Maybe you will meet me and catch me out as being less than perfect and that will validate your experience. Maybe you have overcome challenges too and you have tools that set you up for success. That's great too. Please share them with me and as many people as you can.

Mental health challenges are something that I believe that we are all faced with at varying points in our lives. When we are faced with challenges, it can often feel like a lonely place to be and that can serve to deepen the feelings that we associate to the experience. Counselling works for some but for me all it served to do was to enable me to re-live traumatic experiences and help me to find excuses and reasons as to why I would always be stuck. This had a hugely negative impact on me and made matters worse.

We tend to go to medical professionals for a solution to fix problems and that can land us with labels of what is wrong that are hard to shift. In my experience, I haven't been offered real solutions, I have just been offered drugs to mask the issue and counselling to focus on the issue. NLP and coaching are not therapy. Coaching holds tools and techniques that help you to move from where you are now to where you want to be. NLP helps to rewire the neural pathways in our brain. Learning NLP helped me to understand myself on a deeper level, to understand the strategies I was running that were setting me up for success and to change the things that weren't. It has made such a profound difference to my life that I have chosen to train to the highest level in order to be the best that I can be for my clients, my students, my family and for myself.

Whether I am working with individuals or businesses, it is important to me to understand your end goal. What I offer is to help you to find your route to success, making sure it is aligned to what is important to you, a by-product of that is improved mental fitness.

I didn't much like the labels of 'illness' or 'disorder' when it came to seeking professional help for what was not working well for me. In all honesty, looking back, at that day at the doctors, I think I just needed someone to listen and to have a good cry.

I can offer some tips of wisdom from things that have helped me along my journey but, I am not here to give you another external reference point and tell you what to do. My role, as your coach, is to help you to build upon the resources I believe you already have within you, to make the changes that you know you want. My role as your coach is to encourage you to dream big and to get crystal clear on what it is that you want. When challenges arise, my role as your coach is to help you brighten the spark within you and help you to achieve the success that you desire.

That success could be in the form of tidying a pile of paperwork you couldn't previously face, making a sale or getting that huge promotion, or moving into your dream home. It is not for me to define what that success looks like. Your dreams are yours, and yours alone.

If you are interested in knowing more about my story or would like to explore how NLP and Coaching could help you and/or your team. Please reach out!

Caroline Martin, Leadership Coach and NLP Trainer

Website: www.enablingwings.com

LinkedIn: www.linkedin.com/in/enablingwings

CHAPTER 23

Living Someone Else's Life: A Journey to Authenticity

By Dunja Radosavljevic

Introduction: The Illusion

Have you ever felt like you're living someone else's life, as if you've slipped into a role that doesn't truly fit you? This sensation of wearing an ill-fitting suit is more common than we might realize, especially when there's a stark disconnect between who we are and how we present ourselves. The dissonance can show up in various aspects of our lives, but it's most visible when it comes to self-actualization in our professional career or business.

Navigating a career path that feels unfulfilling is challenging when you're following established norms and rules that go against your internal needs and desires. You might have started with high hopes, climbing the corporate ladder with a vision of success shaped by societal expectations and external benchmarks. Initially, the ascent seemed like the right path—promotions, accolades, and financial rewards often feel amazing in the moment. However, over time, you realize that despite reaching coveted milestones, your soul yearns for something deeper and more meaningful. The well-trodden route that others aspire to starts to feel like a constricting framework rather than the path to fulfillment.

Similar things can happen if you have your own business and are an entrepreneur already. You may struggle to align your vision and unique gifts with the practicalities of making money and positioning yourself as an expert in a crowded marketplace. Conventional marketing and sales tactics that once seemed effective may begin to feel increasingly misaligned with your values and integrity. Even though you are generating revenue, these methods can clash with your core beliefs, leading to a sense of dissatisfaction. The initial excitement of creating real impact starts to wane, leaving you questioning whether you're on the right path.

This questioning is actually a good thing although it feels like frustration and discontent. But this type of discontent is full of creative potential. It's acting as a wake-up call urging you to reevaluate where you stand and what direction you're taking. It nudges you to the crucial step towards true fulfillment: the shedding of that ill-fitting costume that's not yours and the reclaiming of your authenticity.

A Personal Awakening: The Spark of Realization

For me, this moment of realization came unexpectedly in 2015. I stumbled upon an advertisement for a coaching program that promised to help individuals manifest their highest potential. The ad featured a remarkable woman who spoke about innovative tools to awaken your deepest dreams and reach your highest goals such as visualization, questioning limiting beliefs, and transforming what holds us back from stepping into it. This ad ignited a fire in my belly, making me realize that my journey was missing something essential.

I had always been passionate about personal development. From reading *The Celestine Prophecy* to *The Path Less Traveled* and *The Alchemist*, I had immersed myself in a world of deep psychology, spirituality, magic, and manifestation. My interest in these subjects began in my twenties, and coupled with reading books by Jung, Froid, Adler and many other psychologists and personal development masters, it created fertile ground for the coaching idea to land, grow and thrive. Coaching really felt like a natural progression and something I was waiting for a long time – a way to combine all my gifts, knowledge, interests and expertise to truly make an impact in this world.

At the time, I was working as a Marketing and Brand Manager, climbing the corporate ladder in prestigious organizations like Fortune 500 companies and the United Nations. On the surface, it seemed like an ideal path. I built marketing and communication departments, launched high-profile PR campaigns, and represented major organizations. Yet, despite these accomplishments, I felt unfulfilled and frankly - bored.

I craved something deeper and more exciting—something that would set my soul on fire. The prospect of coaching offered that. It promised a journey toward my true self and my authentic story, contrasting sharply with the cookie-cutter corporate path I was on. Plus the opportunity to make a great deal of impact in the world – impact in other people's lives - something that excited me beyond belief. It didn't hurt that it would come with lucrative earnings while being able to have time and family freedom. The idea was irresistible.

The Disillusionment: Facing the Reality of a Broken Dream

When I saw that ad, I immediately subscribed to the coach's email list and followed her diligently for four months. When she launched her one-year coaching academy, it seemed like the perfect opportunity. With my family selling our apartment, I was able to make a significant financial investment in the program. It was the largest commitment I had ever made.

However, the reality of the program was a stark contrast to what I had envisioned. Instead of a transformative experience with personalized attention, the program turned out to be generic and cookie-cutter, with content easily available online or on YouTube. The coaching calls were brief and impersonal, often no more than a few minutes per participant, and the program, designed to serve 300 women, offered little in terms of meaningful support.

I felt deceived and disheartened. The program had promised a space for deep growth and personalized attention but instead taught manipulative sales techniques and aggressive marketing tactics that conflicted with my values. And the curriculum did not address deeper internal blocks that I, and many other women there faced, such as being publicly visible for the first time, writing social media content that sells, and stepping into a leadership role and the face of our business as a sole proprietor.

Despite these shortcomings, my calling to coaching grew stronger. It was as though destiny was urging me to embrace my unique path. By midyear, I realized that this academy was moving me further from my true desires, so I made the difficult decision to leave, even though it meant walking away from my investment. This choice required bravery I didn't know I possessed and taught me to trust my intuition, even when it seemed irrational to others.

A Transformative Experience: Intuition and Insight

Before leaving the academy, I had a transformative experience during a practice coaching session with a colleague. Instead of following the prescribed methods, I followed my intuition, which led to a profound moment of insight. My colleague was struggling with taking on the role of a CEO of a large sustainable business—a position she felt was the right next step for her.

Instead of using standard mindset reframing techniques, I decided to focus on her feelings. When she expressed that she felt confined and limited imagining herself in that CEO role, we uncovered a crucial realization: she was pursuing this only to fulfill her father's legacy, and not her own. This emotional exploration led her to recognize that she wanted to travel and experience life before taking on such a heavy responsibility, and she would allow herself to decide if she would even do that in the future. The freedom and aliveness in her were palpable and I knew I was onto something. This realization empowered her to step away from other people's expectations and pursue what truly resonated with her. It was this unexpected breakthrough that inspired the creation of my own transformational coaching methodology.

The Birth of the Emotional Release Process (ERP)

Inspired by this profound experience, I developed the Emotional Release Process (ERP), a groundbreaking technique that fuses emotional exploration with cognitive questioning. ERP is designed to uncover and address the root cause of clients' struggles, offering instant energetic relief, helping them dismantle false identities that may be blocking their true selves.

As I delved into my process, each layer revealed deeper insights and allowed me to peel back more and more societal expectations and imposed identities I wasn't consciously aware I was adhering to. The technique enabled me to confront and release internal barriers, shifting my focus from conforming to aligning with my own authentic vision. By addressing and healing these core issues that ERP uncovered, I found the courage to redefine my approach to business, making choices that were in harmony with my true self.

One of the most significant impacts of ERP has been its role in my own financial success. By aligning my business practices, mindset and body with my authentic desires, I was able to achieve substantial income growth. I tripled my income three years in a row, proving that ERP not only provides internal reconnection to self but also assists you in hitting your income goals fast. Through ERP, I was able to build a coaching business that reflected my vision and values, serving over 100 clients and achieving significant financial success because I was no longer tethered to outdated or misaligned business strategies and methods. My self-trust returned and I was using it abundantly.

I am immensely proud of my journey, especially given that only about 10% of entrepreneurs make it past the one-year mark, and only 2-3% achieve sustainable income. I am proud that I didn't give up when that program fell short of my expectations and that I trusted my intuition to forge a new path. My work now empowers women to shed their identity masks, embrace their authentic selves, and step into powerful versions of who they are meant to be, so they can earn the money they desire, surpass their income ceiling and create generational wealth.

The Impact of Upbringing: Uncovering Hidden Challenges

However, my story doesn't end here. While shifting inner blocks, I came to a profound understanding that would elevate both my business and personal life, but only after confronting a difficult truth. Doing the work helped me see that I grew up in a family with narcissistic traits, and many of the toxic behaviors I accepted as normal were rooted in this upbringing. This realization revealed why stepping into leadership and authority roles had been so challenging for me and many of the women I work with. Our upbringing conditioned us to be obedient and avoid rocking the boat, which made it harder to embrace our true selves and the creative leadership required for the role of a sole proprietor and business owner.

Narcissistic parents often use their children to satisfy their own needs and desires, leaving the children to grow up without the freedom, love, and safety needed for authentic development. In my case, my parents used me as a tool for their own battles and ambitions, which created a deep disconnect between my true self and the person I was expected to be. It was no surprise that I felt like I was living someone else's dreams and struggled with authenticity and leadership in my business. That's what I was programmed for.

Facing this truth about my parents was challenging, but essential for my growth. Recognizing how it affected my mental health and business, I had to accept this impact and learn to move through it. It took some time to break free from unhealthy beliefs and patterns, but my unwavering desire to uncover my true identity as a powerful creator and leader kept me going. Using my ERP method, I identified and healed subconscious negative self-talk that had been holding me back from stepping into my power, which I couldn't release even after years of therapy.

This breakthrough and realignment to self, was such a significant victory, and it saved me from spiraling into deeper mental health challenges, while allowing me to create a solid foundation for my new empowered business owner identity.

The Role of the Nervous System: Aligning to Success

My healing journey provided an opening to another crucial awareness – the significant role of the nervous system and our body in entrepreneurial success. It highlighted the profound connection between the nervous system and our ability to manifest goals and manage money and wealth. Our nervous system serves as a gatekeeper for our senses and perception, influencing whether we thrive or struggle. Stress stored in the nervous system, regardless of its origin, can severely impact our capacity to welcome, hold, and manage more success and money. This can make it difficult to achieve consistent financial growth and expansion.

In my experience, releasing stress from the nervous system and aligning it with my income goals allowed me to overcome past traumas and embrace my next level income with ease. The stress that was blocking me in many cases wasn't directly related to money; it stemmed from lack of love and appreciation in those early years, creating a scarcity mentality that was affecting my choices in business.

When essential elements to a supportive child rearing are missing, people grow into adults who don't feel worthy or deserving of success. And that blocks them from welcoming and attracting financial abundance even after investing a lot of hard work and effort in their passion business.

By addressing stored stress and realigning the nervous system with my income goals, I developed the confidence and courage to move beyond others' expectations and build a business reflective of my true values and desires. This shift led to consistent financial growth, and I began attracting clients who were just as committed and devoted to making their dreams happen as I was. Ones who had overcome a lot yet still kept their focus on their vision and their North Star.

In my wealth coaching practice today, I always start my one-on-one work with clients by aligning their nervous systems to their income and wealth goals. This alignment ensures that their business strategies, marketing, and sales tactics work harmoniously, leading to effortless results.

When your nervous system is in tune with success, stepping into authority and achieving high revenue becomes straightforward. Then there's a need to make only small tweaks in sales copy, messaging and offer/product suite to explode your revenue beyond what you thought possible.

My clients quickly achieve consistent $10K, $20K, $30K months, break six and multiple six figures, and reach personal milestones such as buying homes, cars, luxury vacations, and private schools for their kids. Most importantly, they shed their masks and start living according to their own desires and expectations, feeling truly alive, connected, and free. And this makes my heart sing.

Families thriving because one person decides to go all in on themselves and their authentic desires.

Celebrating Success: Living Your Authentic Life

My path has been winding and fraught with challenges. I began by feeling like an ugly duckling, wearing a mask of success while struggling internally. It wasn't until I deconstructed the person I thought I should be and embraced my authentic self that I found my true path to success and financial abundance. This journey has been transformative, and I am immensely proud of the progress I've made

I feel grateful to have the opportunity to guide, inspire, and help other incredible women succeed in their businesses, and I am excited for you to embark on your own journey toward authentic success and fulfillment.

Living someone else's life is exhausting. It's time to shed that costume and step into your own skin. The world is waiting for the real you.

Lessons Learned

Here are the key lessons I've gathered on my journey, tailored especially for female entrepreneurs seeking to achieve higher income goals and create lasting wealth:

1. **Trust Your Intuition:** Your inner voice is a powerful guide. Trusting your instincts, even when it means stepping away from commitments that no longer align with your vision, leads you to your true path. My choice to leave the coaching academy, despite the investment, underscores the importance of listening to that inner guidance.

2. **Authenticity Over Conformity**: True fulfillment and success come from embracing who you truly are. Avoid cookie-cutter approaches and manipulative tactics that clash with your values. Instead, honor your authentic self and courageously pave a path that reflects your vision, no matter how different or unconventional it might seem to others.
3. **Align Your Nervous System to Wealth:** Addressing past stress and limiting beliefs in your nervous system is crucial for unlocking high income potential. By using the Emotional Release Process (ERP) to release past influences, I experienced profound personal and professional growth fast (and this isn't sitting for months on your therapist's couch analyzing the past till the cows come home – it's shifting precise experiences out of your body and energy field fast so they no longer affect you or your money flow).
4. **Listen To Your Genius:** Design a business according to what resonates deeply to your values and aspirations, rather than adhering to others' expectations or templates. Trusting my genius and my connection to Divine/Source/Universe/God, allowed me to develop a methodology that worked for me and now effectively serves my clients, leading to fast change they can't encounter anywhere else. Your uniqueness is exactly what your clients need and crave.
5. **Celebrate Your Achievements**: Cherish and celebrate every success, no matter how small. Recognizing your accomplishments helps sustain motivation and confidence,

paving the way for continued growth and abundance. And don't be afraid to seek help for accountability and transformation. Having a friendly ear to bounce off ideas and shift energy and stress holding you back, is essential if you want to achieve rapid business growth, fast results and position yourself as a significant player in the marketplace.

My journey has taught me that living authentically requires both courage and self-awareness. By embodying your true self and embracing nervous system alignment, you can build a fulfilling career and an abundant bank account, while having fun and feeling joyful and purposeful every day.

If you'd like to connect further and explore how you can explode your business through my coaching support, please follow this link or QR code:

Linktree: www.linktr.ee/dunjarado

CHAPTER 24

By Sara Alexander

Failure

I always knew I was expected to achieve great things; my teachers saw the potential, my parents had high hopes, and I knew I was fairly intelligent; so why did it always appear I had to work harder than my peers? Everyone else always seemed to just get it, but I found I needed to know all the details and even then, I couldn't recall things when put on the spot. Yet I could recall details from when I was really young. This always left me feeling 'I'm not good enough, why doesn't my brain remember'! I didn't realise then that I was a visual learner; I would imagine what my notes looked like but struggled to remember the details. I often felt stupid.

I've always been caring; I recall always wanting to help others and a psychological test at school indicated I would suit Social Work, Paramedic and caring type roles, meaning I could help others to feel better about themselves. However, I hadn't done as well as expected in my exams, possibly because I couldn't revise, as nothing seemed to be retained in my brain, so what was the point? I either know it or I don't. Following my slightly disappointing GCSE results, I was lucky to be accepted onto a Health & Social Care course. I was so pleased that my potential was recognised.

Just before I was due to start college, I discovered I was pregnant at the age of 15. The 'father' was 6 years older than me (I now realise how inappropriate this was), had been to prison and was not someone I wanted to be tied to for the rest of my life, even though I quite liked the 'thrill' of a 'bad-boy'. However, I now know this was me seeking that dopamine reward. We'd been together for around a year and as I knew he wasn't 'right' for me, I had tried to end the relationship before discovering my pregnancy. It was important to me to consider my longer-term future; I was lucky enough to be supported with this decision and so I decided to have a termination. Some saw it as courageous, but to me it was a no brainer, I was only 15 and I was about to start a course I had worked hard for and was lucky to get on to. My future was at stake and at that age, it didn't include a baby or an unhealthy relationship.

I started the course and loved it, apart from the coursework. I was able to undertake work experience in a hospital which was so rewarding, but very tiring. As the demand for coursework became more of a struggle for me to keep up with, I started a summer job in a call centre and decided to leave my college course halfway through. Yet another academic failure in my life. I spent the next 10 years working in each department of the company, feeling stuck and bored, whilst fantasising about winning the lottery.

During this time, I moved to a different town, supporting my then partner in their apprenticeship. We had a home and mortgage together; I thought my life was mapped out for me. However, in 2001, after only living together for a year, they suddenly announced one evening that they were leaving, without giving any explanation as to why. This hit me like the proverbial tonne of bricks! I felt abandoned/stranded (as he took our only car), lost and broken. It felt I had no way out and this culminated in what I flippantly describe as a somewhat 'feeble' suicide attempt. Looking back, as serious as this was, I actually laugh over the method I chose; I tried to down some paracetamol with neat vodka, took a few diazepam and jumped down my short flight of stairs. I was taken to hospital and following my brief overnight stay, I was supported by friends and family. Luckily, I didn't experience any lasting physical damage, and I just picked myself up and got on with my life again, after a lot of months of crying of course. I did speak to a counsellor afterwards, but I didn't feel I needed to keep talking about the past as that was just what happened, so I didn't pursue it further. I realise now, that I may have been able to clear some of the beliefs that this left me with, I just didn't see it as traumatic and was told to just get on with it, so that's what I did.

Control (or lack of)

About a year later, I met back up with someone I had known in my late teens when I was working in a village pub. He was also what you could call another 'bad boy'; as I was somewhat of a conformist to rules etc and because he broke all of those, it was exciting! Unfortunately, over the course of about 4 years, the relationship became more and more abusive and controlling. I had always wondered why people stayed when their relationship wasn't working and every month when he was abusive, I'd pack up my things and go back home, saying I won't take it anymore! However, as is often the case with those who display such behaviours, he'd then work his magic of contrition, and I'd go back for more. I always had an unwritten line drawn that if he physically punched me, then that was it! However, he did everything but that. I recall many a time when I'd complain to a friend and they'd say, "I've heard enough now, just leave", so I didn't bother telling anyone anymore. Even a parent once said to him "oh you know what she's like, it's her PMT, she'll be back"!!

The relationship finally came to an end after he had tried strangling me as I was about to drive him to an appointment. I just about managed to get him out of my car and my only escape was to follow a police car to the station, with him following me in his car. I guess you could say it took courage to go into a police station, I was petrified so it was my only option. It also took a lot of courage to share the level of control and abuse he'd subjected me too, but I felt like a fool hearing it out loud.

Why on earth did I put up with it and keep going back for more? I think at the time, I thought that I could be the one to help him to change, but I didn't realise he had to want to change yet he wasn't able to.

Just before this, in 2003, I had a car accident (the abusive partner was in the car with me at the time). I wasn't seriously injured, but when I finally started to receive acupuncture treatment for my whiplash injury, a year later I may add, I was signed off work and told to not do anything! This was hell for me as I'd always been socially active and by then I was living on my own, in a different town to friends and family, without a car. I felt very much alone and as though I had no control over my life, it became so monotonous and empty. Whilst signed off work in 2005, I was also made redundant from the job I'd been in for the past 10 years, which can be a really difficult time for some, but my only commitment was paying my mortgage. After my initial fear of the future, I saw it as a kick up the rear to finally get into a job that I found fulfilling and to give my life some purpose for me!

Turning point 1

This is where I actually felt courageous and truly excited about my future for the first time in my life. I joined a job training programme that meant I could earn a full wage, so could still afford to pay my mortgage and obtain a degree, whilst working full-time over 2 years. It was scary going back to learning, given my previous 'struggles' with coursework but I revelled at the opportunity. To say this new vocation gave me purpose was an understatement. Whilst the academic side was still a big struggle,

I really enjoyed the training and supporting others to improve their lives, and it felt like I had found my true calling.

It was also during these 2 years training, that I met the person I went on to marry. I knew I wasn't always the easiest to get on with, opinionated, wouldn't stand for crap (whilst always still standing for crap), but I felt I had finally met someone who supported and accepted me for who I was.

The next few years saw me finishing my training and getting a degree. I moved into a role that involved delivering cognitive behavioural therapy group work to those who had problematic behaviour and found a love for group work. However, I often felt hypocritical telling others how to improve their relationships and lives when I was falling flat myself. We married and after some difficulties due to me having endometriosis, we finally managed to get pregnant and have a child. I had wondered if my earlier termination impacted on this and started to experience those negative guilt feelings that can spiral downwards. Unfortunately, the constant disagreements continued and although I felt I had settled with my lot as he was a 'good man', I still wasn't happy. I still felt my life was lacking, always searching for external sources of validation, wanting more money/comfort/freedom in life.

I had numerous failed attempts at job promotion. Attending a work conference, I realised that I had all the characteristics of dyslexia, so I had an assessment, and I was diagnosed as dyslexic. I remember telling a parent, who said don't tell anyone or you will be discriminated against. However, what I hadn't known was that it meant I could have viewed interview questions beforehand, which would give my brain a fighting chance of not shutting down when under pressure. Then, not long after returning from maternity leave, I had to step down from the job I loved as it included working evenings which I was no longer able to do, as the additional support I had with childcare couldn't continue. It was all so unfair and sent me into a real self-pity party.

After lots of attempts of trying to get my relationship back on track and trying to feel happier and more content, things didn't change. We had conversations and decided that we would be able to be better parents and happier if we separated. I remember feeling a huge sense of relief, as well as fear for how I would possibly support myself and my child alone. Fortunately, it was all amicable which helped, but it was yet another failure and setback in my life.

Big changes ahead

At this time, when faced with having to support myself and my child alone, I went for a job promotion. This time, I was able to share about dyslexia and so I was able to view the questions in advance. This gave my brain the chance to reflect on all my previous experience and I absolutely smashed the interview and was subsequently offered the job. I was thrilled, I felt as though this was exactly what I needed to achieve the bright, abundant future I envisaged. However, whilst still living with my ex-partner and dealing with finding a new home, the job and separation (or rather fear of the future) was all too much for me. I was totally overwhelmed.

I remember feeling at my lowest, crying most days, not coping, feeling stupid and like a failure. I spoke out to anyone who was willing to listen, but it didn't seem to make a difference as nothing changed. I'd always advocated to anyone struggling to speak about it, not bottle it up and solutions will be found. Well, that wasn't how it was for me. There was no respite at work or home, I was living in a nightmare. I remember I had a counselling session where the initial questionnaires indicated a high level of depression, but I wouldn't accept that, as I knew it was situational and that if I resolved the situation, I knew I would be fine.

So, I took what many described as a brave decision to step down from the promotion that I'd always wanted, regardless of the lower pay when I really needed more as I was going it alone. Unfortunately, it took another 6 months before I was able to step down, as Covid had hit, and my replacement wasn't able to start immediately. However, knowing there was a light at the end of the tunnel meant I could keep going – just!

Self-compassion

In going back to my previous role, it yet again felt like I'd failed. I kept wondering why me, why is it always so hard for me to succeed, why do I always struggle so much? A colleague had shared their experiences of having ADHD and it got me reflecting. I'd also been pursuing an Autism diagnosis for my child, much to the dispute of their father. So, as I always did so well, I researched and spoke to many people about Neurodivergence. Everything resonated so loudly for me that I had to find out about myself.

I'd say that one of the biggest lightbulb moments for me was when I finally got my diagnosis. So much about my experiences in relationships, at school, at work all started to make sense. I wasn't useless, broken, defective, or a failure!! I had ADHD, it just meant my brain processed things differently to those with a Neurotypical brain. The biggest thing that I wanted to work on, and change was how negatively I spoke to myself. I was always saying "oh stupid bitch" or "ffs, why am I so stupid". I could finally give myself a break, although it was far easier said than done.

I left the job security and went to work for a charity who I believed would be far more compassionate and understanding about my needs, as I was supporting others who had all manner of support needs around their emotional well-being. What I hadn't counted on was that working from home meant I didn't have the colleagues around me for connection and support and I was lonely. I flitted between relationships, trying to find someone who would accept me and my 'quirks'. I knew I wanted and deserved more from life. I also wanted to improve my income and help as many people as I could, without being confined by so many restrictions and limitations.

Healing

At this time of ticking along, feeling resentful and wanting more, even though I had no time or additional resources, I attended a 3-day online masterclass about Belief Coding® by Jessica Cunningham, that popped up whilst doom-scrolling on social media and it totally changed my life, so much for the better. I'd never heard of this before, but I did know about positive psychology, neuroscience, and how trapped negative experiences show up in the body, so I was intrigued at how this mixed modality could cause such a significant, instant change. I knew I wanted to help others initially, but I didn't realise I had so much to heal myself. In one masterclass session, I cleared a nagging neck pain that had been 'trapped' since my car accident, just my subconscious didn't reveal that to my conscious.

This was the perfect opportunity for me to finally believe and invest in myself and my family's future. With a fire ignited in my solar plexus, I signed up immediately. Regardless of all the self-doubt life instilled in me and thinking I never have any spare time, how am I going to do this and all the other fear-based negative thoughts that entered my head. However, I learned that I need to feel them, to heal them. I am still working on them; it's quite a long list and I deal with one belief at a time. I still remember thinking wow, I really can heal me and the world with this modality that gets right to the root of any problem, everyone will be begging me to help them. Of course, there was resistance from friends and family, but I had found a group of like-minded individuals who also wanted to help others. I had finally found my inspiration and the means to create a huge impact on the people around me and create security for my future.

Inspired action

Of course, as I mentioned, all the old thoughts returned of self-doubt, self-sabotage, procrastination, overwhelm, fear – of success and failure. I knew I needed to keep at it, but as a working parent with ADHD, it has been a struggle; but I'm not going to lie, I've thrived on my rekindled love of learning and stretching myself, finding something that I'm passionate about and most importantly, being a positive role-model for my child.

I'm proud to say that becoming an accredited Belief Coding® facilitator and training as a Master Belief Coding® facilitator – meaning I can deliver sessions to groups, has finally rid me of those subconsciously self-imposed beliefs around being a failure, stupid, not deserving more, who am I to help others; well let me tell you, I now see it takes those who have experienced these to really understand what can help others. The techniques I use include elements of EFT/tapping, positive psychology, kinesiology, and NLP, which are scientifically and spiritually backed. All experiences we go through get stored in the 'soma', our body and they show up in ways that our subconscious is trying to keep us safe, resulting in overwhelm, procrastination, self-sabotage, as well as health issues and pain. This can clear those and get you back to living the life you desire and deserve.

I've gone on to undertake Breakthrough Breathwork training, which is amazing at allowing you to release stored up, subconscious limitations; I regularly practise yoga and meditation, my favourite is an app called the Insight Timer where I select what resonates with me at the end of each day. I have completed my Reiki level 1, level 2 and now I am qualified as a Reiki Master which means I can attune others to Reiki. It's an amazing energy that really shifts what we don't always realise we are storing within our body that is limiting us.

I am an accredited Inner Freedom coach and have inspired clients to embrace their courage and take inspired action to achieve the life they envisage, without sabotaging it subconsciously. I am a certified Chakra healing practitioner; trained in intergenerational trauma; trauma-certified coach, and a certified mental health first aider. I really do understand that it is not as simple as 'just do it'!

I am so excited to meet others who may have experienced or felt anything similar to what I have shared with you, whom I can support to reach their full potential. I have explored many modalities, following a career delivering cognitive behavioural technique programmes to empower people to take inspired action to regain control of their lives and bring in some connection, joy, gratitude and be authentically themselves.

If you want to improve your life, get rid of limitations, clear blocks, authentically be who you know you are, and live the life you know you deserve, get in touch! I'd love to support you on your journey towards courageously embracing your authentic self.

You can find out more about me and my work at:

Linktree: www.linktr.ee/sarabcmentoring

CHAPTER 25

By Sabrina Ellis

Can You See Me?

My first name was given to me by my mother, and my Welsh surname is a choice I made out of love. Together, they reflect who I am and who I've chosen to become. My hazel eyes symbolise the openness and trust I offer when I look at you. My curly hair, a part of me I cherish, is a gift from my dual heritage—Black Jamaican and White British parents.

But imagine what lies beneath this introduction. Behind my name is a story of trauma and pain, embedded in my journey as I walked through life with a maiden name that never quite fit. Growing up brown in a world that often sees only black or white, I struggled with a lack of identity. My hair, too, tells a story: its length reflects my mental health, my grief and my ability to cope at different moments in time.

This is only the surface. Let me take you deeper.

Alone in the Dark

At 37 years old, I am still afraid of the dark. I sleep with the landing light on, jump at loud noises, and feel my stomach sink when I see smudges on windows. These marks remind me of my childhood, where I would hear the terrifying thuds of a fist hitting my mom and see the ear marks left on windows by the alcohol-soaked man who stole my childhood.

People often comment on how much I change my hair. New styles, new colours, they assume it's self-care but my hair is more than just fashion. When it's long, I'm happy. When it's short, I'm lost. Unwashed hair means I'm depressed, and mid-length hair shows I'm healing.

Living alone after my brother and sister left was isolating. I would listen intently to the voices in the house, trying to gauge my next move, or whether I should stay perfectly still. I longed for stability, for a safe space where my mom wouldn't scream or be covered in bruises, where no men would be left alone with me. My mom had a big heart, full of love, but she was consumed by a dark, heavy cloud; one that I could never penetrate, no matter how hard I tried. This cloud brought her nothing but pain, a torment she lived with day and night.

Despite everything, I stood by my mom until her dying breath and even beyond. Some would say I was a child carer to an alcoholic; I say I was a daughter who loved her mother unconditionally.

Living Life on Autopilot

As a child, people would say I was mature for my age. As an adult, they call me strong. Both are exhausting labels. From as far back as I can remember, I've always needed a plan, survival depended on it. And so, I kept moving forward, one step after the other, living life on autopilot. When my mind is busy, I'm too scared to stand still.

At 22, I graduated from university as a Registered Mental Health Nurse (RMN) with my two beautiful boys by my side. Being a single mom wasn't part of the plan, neither was being pregnant and homeless. But after my dad disowned me at 18 for refusing an abortion, I had to keep going. I paused my nursing course to support my mom through home detoxes, even though it was discouraged and I worked to bring in extra income. People made jokes about it taking me five years to finish a three-year course, saying I could have been a doctor if I hadn't kept having children. They said it was foolish to take driving lessons while living in a women's safe house without a car. If we don't take the first step, if we don't set our own goals and strive forward, how will we ever discover what's truly possible?

I became an RMN to help my mom, but soon realised that everyone's journey is shaped by their individual challenges. Years passed working on mental health wards, where I empowered others to find their voices. But outside of work, I had no space for my own voice. I was so busy surviving that I didn't see the storm cloud forming over my own heart, denying me peace and happiness. I kept myself occupied, extra shifts, looking after other people's children and completing chores on my days off. Never allowing myself to stop, not even long enough for a good night's sleep.

Until one day, I sat on Miami South Beach for Micha's 21st birthday and she asked me a question that finally turned off my autopilot. For the first time, I stopped. I thought. Most importantly, I began to change.

I started to see the cloud of postnatal depression that weighed me down after the split from my partner during my second pregnancy. I could see the storm from my past, filled with trauma and pain. The triggers of Post-Traumatic Stress Disorder (PTSD) that haunted me day and night were now clearer. Micha helped me realise what she could already see: that I was someone who could socially engage and seem like a person people wanted to spend time with, but also someone who could be withdrawn and riddled with anxiety.

My boys would stay with their dad and his girlfriend on weekends, the woman he had been seeing since my first pregnancy. After she, not him, collected them at the door to their building, I would sit in my car, gripped by panic attacks. I would cry uncontrollably, the pain in my heart unbearable. Then I would wipe away my tears, put my mask back on and head to work, where I would help others in need. I didn't know how to help myself, so I just kept going.

This pattern lasted for years. Taking antidepressants, coping by helping others, never learning how to be still or kind to myself. After a serious incident at work, bathrooms became unbearable for me. I would sit outside the bathroom door while my children bathed, and my sister would wash my hair in a plastic tub in the living room. I kept seeing my dead patient on the floor, everywhere I went. I knew she wasn't really there, but she was! Her eyes open, staring at me. Around others I was seen as strong, but no one noticed the mental ill health that I kept hidden. Even if they did, no one ever told me.

Learning to Calm My Own Storm

From a young age, I've always been quick to think of solutions. I remember one Christmas morning when I was about 11 or 12 years old, the phone rang, and it was Leanne. She wanted us to open our presents together. I smiled with joy, taking turns to unwrap gifts and laugh together. What Leanne didn't know was that the only presents I opened were in my imagination. This memory, the first of me being solution focused, unknowingly set the stage for overcoming one challenge after another throughout my life.

Fast forward to 2011, when I returned from Miami, I made the difficult decision to reduce my full-time contract at an NHS Psychiatric Intensive Care Unit (PICU) to part-time. This change allowed me to start taking antidepressants, not just for chronic nerve pain from a work-related injury, but also to lift my mood. The extra time with my children was precious. We enjoyed after-school trips to the park, picnics on the grass, and indoor picnics under a den we would build out of furniture and sheets on rainy days. For the first time in a long while, I began to laugh and smile again.

However, financial pressures meant that I couldn't sustain part-time hours for long. After six months, I returned to full-time shift work. The symptoms of PTSD persisted, coupled with a long commute, so I sought support from my Trust's Occupational Health. Despite being told I didn't require additional support, I knew what I was experiencing was beyond my capacity for self-help. I eventually moved to a new NHS trust closer to home, whilst ensuring there was no conflict of interest with my mom accessing services or care.

This new role brought opportunities, including appropriate support at work. I was referred for Eye Movement Desensitisation and Reprocessing (EMDR) therapy for my PTSD. This therapy helped me process traumatic memories that had become mentally stuck. The sessions were intense, often leaving me with migraines and unable to drive for 24 hours afterward. Around this time, approximately nine months after the workplace incident that triggered my PTSD, I attended Coroner's court with my old trust and colleagues. It was stressful, but I felt proud to represent the patient we had lost.

Work however, presented new challenges. My relationship with my ward manager began to deteriorate, especially when I requested time off or specific shifts to take my son Kaydn to his ongoing medical appointments. Some of these appointments were missed because I couldn't afford the time off unpaid. I longed to provide more holistic care to my family and patients, to see them as more than their labels. Over time, EMDR therapy helped me see things from a different perspective, and gradually, the symptoms I had been struggling with began to ease. Yet, after a transfer to another ward and hospital within the trust was denied, I realised it was time to move on.

I found a new role as a Peripatetic Nurse working in the private sector. It was exhilarating to attend a new nursing home every few days or weeks, identifying their challenges and supporting them in finding sustainable solutions. An 80-bedded nursing home was under an embargo and rated "red" by the Care Quality Commission (CQC), I made it my mission to turn things around. On my first day, I took down the hot drinks order of each staff member. When one care assistant pretended to faint, I quickly went into risk assessment mode, only to realise it was a joke. She laughed and said, "No nurse has ever made me a drink before." I replied, "You better get used to it," and from that moment, I knew I was where I needed to be.

Within a short time, the team asked me to become a permanent member and I proudly accepted the role of Unit Manager, later becoming Deputy Home Manager. Together, we focused on improving the quality of care for residents and the wellbeing of each team member. My solution-focused thinking was bursting with ideas, and the team was integral to bringing them to life. After a year of hard work, including sleepovers with our night team on Fridays, we improved the standards of care and support for residents, achieving a "green" rating from the CQC. We even celebrated with a company paid night out, something unheard of before. The team may have thought I was solely there to help them, but they were helping me, too.

During this time, I also made personal strides. I was finally able to return to swimming, a solitary activity that brought me peace. It was just me and the water, the noise and the movement soothing my soul. I started running again, raising funds for charities and local causes, participating in my first half marathon at the Great North Run, an incredible experience. Reading was a long-term goal due to my poor memory, something I actively work towards.

At home, I could finally use bathrooms again, a significant improvement from the days when I couldn't even enter one. I still preferred to keep the door open when inside, but I could now enjoy bath time with my sons, playing games and laughing. Planning things to look forward to, whether it was afternoon tea, a night out with my old-school garage ravers or roller-skating with the boys, made my mind feel alive again.

From Love to Loss

As I focused on making happy memories with my boys and balancing health and happiness, life became a joy to live every day. With support from my GP, I gradually reduced and eventually stopped taking antidepressants. I looked forward to new adventures, Disneyland Paris, Pembrokeshire in Wales, Cancun in Mexico, Miami South Beach (a favourite trip with my sister), and Las Vegas in 2014 where I met my future husband. I had never known such happiness and I was grateful every single day.

My life was now filled with love, shared with a man who knew my past but never judged me for it. Instead, he focused on where we were going together as a family. In 2018, Alexander was born, and I became a mom of three boys. During Alexander's pregnancy, I received ongoing support for PTSD symptoms triggered by the traumatic birth of Zion in 2009, who was breech by feet. Even now, Zion is unapologetically authentic and makes an entrance wherever he goes!

Twice, my mom celebrated two years of being alcohol free, I still get reminders from my calendar. She loved a good fuss and her living room would be filled with flowers and balloons delivered by the boys. She would always dress up in her best clothes for the occasion.

At the start of the COVID-19 pandemic, I was asked as an RMN to work at the Nightingale hospital. Having recently gone through my second miscarriage in five months, I was unable to fulfil the duty of care I was trained to provide. Instead, I volunteered to support the mental health and wellbeing of NHS staff from home. By day, I home-schooled the children and by night, I provided support to those on the front line.

One NHS doctor said to me "I felt like she really saw me and understood me. Her consultation style suited me perfectly; she was very warm and listened well. She made me feel like I was strong but also worthy of spending the time I needed to focus on myself and my own wellbeing. She reminded me that I am not just a doctor, I am a human being!"

However, following our third miscarriage in October 2020, which required two blood transfusions and another trip to the operating theatre, I took time out to recover. I felt trapped in my loss, suffocating under the weight of it. This was the first time I shared our baby loss journey with family and friends. I never realised the positive impact this would have. It empowered others to reach out and talk about their losses, which they had held onto internally. I started walking for my well being and sharing this online led to other women caring for their minds after their own losses. At the time, I questioned why this happened to us, but now I see it was preparing me for the future losses to come.

In 2021, we became pregnant again. The pregnancy was debilitating, marked by Severe Symphysis Pubis Dysfunction (SPD), where my pelvis would rotate, causing excruciating pain and reducing my mobility. I went from walking on crutches to being non-weight-bearing in a wheelchair. My dignity seemed to vanish as my husband and eldest boys helped me with personal hygiene and other basic tasks. But it was the little moments, like when my husband let go of the wheelchair during a family walk and we all laughed as I rolled away, that got me through each struggle.

Eventually, the pain became too unbearable, and I activated our emergency care plan, which I had been avoiding due to COVID-19. I was hospitalised and bed-bound on morphine for 10 days. Samuel was born, a healthy 8 lbs 15 oz. I was now a wife and mother of four beautiful boys, and my heart felt complete.

My mobility was still limited, but by the end of March 2022, I was able to drive my automatic car. My mom had been unwell, so we couldn't visit her on Mothering Sunday, nor could we plant any seasonal bulbs over winter due to my pain and reduced mobility. So, on Sunday 3rd April, we decided to buy some daffodils, her favourite flowers and take them to Nanny Pat. That was the last day I woke up smiling. My mom died peacefully on Wednesday, 6th April 2022, just seven days before her 60th birthday. We had been planning a family holiday together for when she got better.

Survival mode kicked in as I supported my sister, brother and children through our grief. My sister, who had faced health challenges all her life, seemed to deteriorate rapidly after our mom's death. On Sunday, 20th November 2022, she was taken to Resus following a suspected asthma attack. On Wednesday, 23rd November 2022, at the age of 41, my sister died.

My sister was my world. I do not understand how we have gone from three to just me.

I feel exhausted. I feel sad. I feel lonely. Repeat.

Embracing a Glimmer of Hope

The world was moving too fast and I struggled to keep up with everything I needed to do, both inside and outside of our home. Arranging two funerals, packing up two homes, and sorting through a lifetime of memories within just six months took its toll. I was broken, feeling alone even in a room full of people. Yet, looking back, I can see that I was never truly alone. I had a great support network that helped me through. The right support can provide a glimmer of hope, even when we feel hopeless. Kiran bought and delivered our food shopping, Stacey looked after baby Samuel, and Chantell and Simone stood by my husband to ensure our boys were supported in their grief. My cousin's Naomi, Amber and Aunty Debbie also remained constant as I tried to catch up while the earth kept spinning.

Living my whole life with my big sister meant that after her death, I needed time to think about how I could continue without her. Unable to solve this problem, I gravitated to the one thing I knew I could do, helping others. In June 2023, we registered NICS Wellbeing CIC, a Community Interest Company. The name 'NICS' holds dual significance: it's a tribute to my sister Nicola, known as Nic, and it stands for Nics Inclusive Coaching and Self-care. With the unwavering support of our volunteer team, we launched the organisation in November 2023.

NICS Wellbeing empowers people with lived experiences of mental health challenges and additional needs to live their best lives. We support vulnerable adults and children with Neuroprofiles through Neurodivergent Coaching, Co-Coaching, reflective practice, listening spaces, child development projects and community events. Funds raised from our paid services, fundraising efforts and grants are reinvested into projects that create possibilities in our community and beyond. We work fluidly, ensuring that the social impact we make aligns with the best interests of those we serve, involving the community every step of the way. Founding NICS Wellbeing has given me a purpose and a way to channel my grief into something positive.

Recently one client wrote to me "Meeting you over the last few months has changed my life. YOU ARE AN ASSET!! The deep sorrow and pain I felt was indescribable… I kept this overwhelming pain inside all this time with no way to heal. Just having you sitting with me has allowed me to exhale. I was able to release how broken I was".

But where am I right now, you may wonder? Eighteen months after my mom died, I reached the limit of my ability to cope on my own. In July 2024, I had a breakdown. I now take antidepressants and I'm working to rebuild the relationships within my household that grief has strained, whilst supporting Kaydn to move away to University. I look forward to being kinder to myself by returning to the water in September to swim regularly, something that has always brought me peace. I'm also exploring ways to strengthen my physical core after the challenges of SPD, as I couldn't engage in rehabilitation at the time. And as for the future, who knows? I may finally run that marathon I've always wanted to do.

Through all of this, I've learned that healing is not a linear process. The journey continues and it's filled with ups and downs. But with the support of my loved ones and the work I'm doing with NICS Wellbeing, I'm beginning to see that there is hope, even in the darkest times.

If you'd like to follow the journey of NICS Wellbeing and see the positive impact we're making, scan the QR code.

NOTES

NOTES

NOTES

NOTES

NOTES

Pro Publishing House

Printed in Great Britain
by Amazon